# PRAISE FOR I/

*"In the Game* is the riveting memoir ᴗᴊ ᴗ ᴗ
blasted down the locked doors that had effectively shut women out
of the practice of law since the writing of the Ten Commandments.
Her strength, her spirit, and her brilliance shine through these
pages and show how it took all of that to overcome the enormous
obstacles put in her way."

> —**Marcia Clark,** author of crime novel *Blood Defense* and
> former O.J. Simpson prosecutor

*"In the Game* offers an insight into a high-stakes legal world and a
lawyer who fought in the trenches."

> —**Geri Spieler,** author of *Taking Aim At The President*

"If you think that Courtroom trials are dull and boring, you haven't
experienced the epee-like skills of Peggy Garrity, acting as a powerful legal advocate for her clients! In covering hundreds of trials, I
have seen the many degrees of lawyering and legal wrangling, and
Ms. Garrity is one of the best. *In the Game* is a great read, and a
great ride . . . with a look into the many facets of a well-lived life
and career."

> —**Mona Shafer Edwards,** Courtroom Illustrator and author of
> *Captured: Inside the World of Celebrity Trials*

*"In the Game* will shed light on the injustices of the justice system and
the ways a strong, determined trial lawyer can make a difference in
her client's life. When I first met Peggy Garrity, I was a broken woman
fighting to protect my severely autistic child. Where other attorneys
saw only obstacles and endless litigation, Peggy found opportunities
and even showed me I could laugh again. To this day if she told me
to 'do cartwheels in the courthouse hallway,' I would. Peggy Garrity
saved our lives."

> —**Elaine Hall,** author, *Now I See the Moon: a Mother, A Son, and
> the Miracle of Autism,* star of the Emmy–award winning HBO
> documentary *Autism: The Musical*

# IN THE GAME

# IN THE GAME

## THE HIGHS AND LOWS OF A TRAILBLAZING TRIAL LAWYER

## PEGGY GARRITY

SHE WRITES PRESS

Published 2016
Printed in the United States of America
ISBN: 978-1-63152-105-8
Library of Congress Control Number: 2016937051

For information, address:
She Writes Press
1563 Solano Ave #546
Berkeley, CA 94707

Cover design © Julie Metz, Ltd./metzdesign.com
Interior design by Tabitha Lahr

She Writes Press is a division of SparkPoint Studio, LLC.

Names and identifying characteristics have been changed to protect the privacy of certain individuals.

"If you don't win, don't come home."

—Marion Fournier Garrity

## DEDICATED TO

Sister Lucille Winnike (Sister Linus),
the first and foremost feminist in my life;

my mother, the original life coach;

and my children, Erin, Colin, Bronwyn, and Seamus,
who took this journey with me.

# AUTHOR'S NOTE

Events and people depicted in this memoir are real and part of my life experience as best I remember them. The cases and characters are in the public legal record as well as in numerous media accounts. Material has been excluded that is confidential under the attorney-client privilege or that violates the right to privacy. Names have been changed where deemed appropriate or where they were not part of the public record.

# CONTENTS

## PART ONE

## PART TWO

## PART THREE

# PROLOGUE

*This will never be me,* I promise my thirteen-year-old self as I watch my mother. It is June 20, 1960. Mom is due to give birth to her ninth child, is perhaps even in the early stages of labor, and is packed for the hospital. Yet tonight she's dressed up and wearing bright red lipstick, hosting a smoky Jesuit cocktail party in the living room. My father, the funeral director in the Mississippi River hamlet of Prairie du Chien, Wisconsin, has invited these priests to watch the televised Floyd Patterson–Ingemar Johannsen heavyweight boxing championship on our flickering black-and-white television. Dad is serving this Roman-collar frat party smoked carp and oysters, cheese, and sausage, properly paired with Wisconsin beer and Irish whiskey.

When a priest jokes that the baby "should be named Floyd Ingemar," the room erupts in laughter, including my mother. I cringe. In this profoundly personal moment, my mother has no privacy or respect in her own living room. Her life is not her own. Even her body seems not to be her own as this roomful of men freely jokes about what is going on inside of it. I am mortified at the changes taking place in my own adolescent body, and I wear heavy sweaters to camouflage the mounting evidence of sexuality that I believe will seal my own fate. My mother's participation in this spectacle confirms my worst suspicions. Women who play by the rules are doomed. What an injustice. I vow then not to let men, marriage, or motherhood take over my life.

I will become a nun.

I will never indulge men the way my mother does.

I will become a doctor, a medical missionary, and travel to faraway places.

Even after I hear my father, oldest brother, and the priests who teach at Campion, the boys' high school, ridicule the nuns as an inside joke, I still think the convent and life as a doctor and medical missionary is my way out.

Until I become pregnant and get married my senior year in college.

When this happens, I promise myself: I still will not surrender my commitment to equality, and my determination to have a professional life. Weighing my options, it dawns on me that perhaps my pursuit of justice should be more direct. And law school, unlike medical school, can be undertaken part-time and at night. So I take the LSAT. Diapers and legal briefs will soon become a way of life.

\*   \*   \*

Women trial lawyers were almost non-existent in 1975 when I started out—so, to get a toehold, I took just about any case that got me into court. I leapt at the counsel and mentoring offered by one of the partners in the firm from which I rented an office. Admission to this unofficial bar meant long hours in the colorful pubs of the Los Angeles South Bay as, to my surprise, I was welcomed into the game.

Finally, I had escaped the entangled traps of culture and Catholicism that I had been so sure had ensnared my mother as I watched her, my father, and the priests in that living room all those years before. However, I would learn firsthand that the pursuit of justice would require me to spend time with people far worse than those priests, and in places much less inviting than the living room of my childhood.

In my first year of practice I successfully defended a flasher named Mr. Cummings (swear to God) in a lurid jury trial for the grand sum of $300. A year later I brought a habeas corpus motion on behalf of would-be presidential assassin Sara Jane Moore, who was serving a life sentence at Terminal Island prison for trying to shoot President Gerald Ford. Twenty years later I represented actress Sondra Locke in a jury trial against Clint Eastwood. I was an adrenaline junkie, and living on the edge was my way of life. I used Chardonnay and martinis to soften the edge. For almost thirty years I rode the highs and lows of the sole practitioner and single mother. And then it all caught up with me.

When I was fifty-seven I nearly died from a ruptured diverticulum that caused sepsis and peritonitis, requiring emergency surgery and two weeks of delirium in ICU. On my first day of semi-consciousness in the hospital, I found myself floating on feelings of relief and surrender: relief from the unrelenting pressure of my life, and peaceful surrender to death if it came.

The law and motherhood had been my life and my love—had shaped my identity—for three decades. I had thrived on the intensity and excitement of going it alone, and even on the struggle for survival. Even when shingles and a destroyed immune system had disabled me seven years earlier, I had jumped right back into a life and litigation practice rife with conflict as soon as I was able. On that earlier occasion of illness, my doctor had counseled me to make serious changes in my life or the universe would make the change for me. It seemed he'd been right; the universe had apparently decided it was time to take over.

As I lay convalescing in my cozy beach house, a dolled-up, double-wide trailer in the Point Dume Club mobile home park overlooking the ocean in Malibu, I was riveted by television footage of the devastating tsunami that devoured a quarter of a million people along the Indian Ocean a few days after Christmas 2004. I identified with those who had been miraculously saved, strained up out of the deadly brew by random branches of palm trees that remained rooted. One man had saved his entire family by tying them to the tops of the trees.

As I watched the coverage, which showed huge elephants walking across downed pillars, as sure-footed and dainty as elite gymnasts in a beam routine, rescuing people from under piles of debris, it seemed to me that the Hindu elephant god Ganesh, the remover of obstacles, was manifest. These mysterious giants went about inspecting and reaching into the rubble without disturbing it or causing cave-ins, deftly using their trunks to locate and rescue trapped survivors. The powerful pachyderms had broken free of their chains and fled to higher ground as the tsunami headed for shore, then returned to help and go where humans and heavy machinery could not.

Two images of Ganesh had greeted me when I awoke in the hospital. A small bronze dancing Ganesh, a gift from my yoga teacher, stood atop a beautiful journal embossed with the elephant god's image, a gift from my daughter. Synchronicity was everywhere I looked.

\*     \*     \*

When my family gathered at my daughter Bronwyn's house for my birthday following my near-death-experience (NDE, as it is commonly called among us Baby Boomers), we sat around a candlelit dining room table that had once been my office conference table—the scene of, as my son Seamus gingerly put it, "a lot of legal pound downs." We reminisced about the years of depositions, trials, research, client sessions, and hasty carry-out lunches and dinners to which the hefty chunk of wood had borne witness. My four children mused about the school assignments they'd completed at that table, occasionally typed by my secretaries Gloria and Karen, who were not infrequently conscripted into service as surrogate mothers. Their reminiscences reminded me of a favorite childhood book, which I must have read to them over a thousand bedtimes: *The Giving Tree*. This old burled wood table, with so much of our history in it, was our version of the tree.

# PART ONE

# CHAPTER 1

# THE FUNERAL
# DIRECTOR'S DAUGHTER

As the third of ten kids in an Irish Catholic family, I was a competitor: determined to be the best at everything I did, and to do everything.

My mother knew being a star was my ticket out—so, intent on sparing me a life of endless childbearing, she pushed me to compete and win in whatever arena I was allowed, including swimming, diving, ice skating, piano, speech, math, and even hula hooping. One day, when I said I didn't want to compete in a ridiculous bicycle rodeo, she insisted, and sent me off with the admonition, "If you don't win, don't come home."

Mom had me competing in any event that would have me. Because most wouldn't. I might jump the hurdles faster than all the boys in the hours before a track meet, but when the actual event started I had to sit in the stands. I was not allowed to play baseball on a real team in the city ballpark, either, even though I hit farther and ran faster than most of the boys.

In sixth grade my mother coached me to become the Crawford County spelling champion; immediately after that win, she started drilling me for the state finals. At the end of a long day, she would call out words from the dictionary from where she lay in bed, and I would chime back from the room I shared with my four younger sisters down the hall: "onomatopoeia: o-n-o-m-a-t-o-p-o-e-i-a; eleemosynary: e-l-e-e-m-o-s-y-n-a-r-y."

I got through several rounds of competition at the state championship—and then, to my disbelief, misspelled a simple word ("destruction" somehow came out as "distruction").

My mother dismissed my disastrous performance, blaming it on the pronouncer. "He was terrible! You spelled it just the way he pronounced it." To my surprise, she suggested shopping was a better use of our time, and indulged me with the purchase of a new beach bag shaped and colored exactly like a watermelon, with a matching towel, along with a huge hot fudge sundae. She didn't seem to care that I hadn't won, and set about to cheer me up by making the most of our trip to the state capitol. My mother just loved getting out of our small town and into the city—any city. My competitions gave her a way to get there.

I grew up on a foundation of unquestioning allegiance to, and love for, the Catholic Church. Starting in first grade at St. John's four-room schoolhouse—sixty-four kids in two classes per room—and continuing through high school at St. Mary's Academy for girls, I went to daily Mass and Communion. At a young age, I experienced a profound and emotional connection to the faith. Sundays, Holy Days, and funerals showcased a lavish Latin liturgy steeped in smoky incense and Gregorian chant. I loved being upstairs singing the dolorous Latin *"Miserere Mei, Deus . . ."* with the choir during funerals my dad handled. I felt like I was sort of his partner.

The funeral business was full of sacred mystery, and we were taught to regard it with reverence. My sister Bridget and I were required to wear skirts if we were ever out in the evening, and all of us were reminded frequently that wherever we went in our town, we represented my dad and his business. Though my gender placed serious limitations on me, I participated in church in every way I could, from singing in the choir to helping the nuns dress the altar and lay out the priest's vestments in the sacristy. Occasionally I even got to place the unconsecrated hosts in the gold chalice that the priests would pray over and raise high above the altar at the Consecration during Mass. My proximity to these ancient rituals set the stage for a lifelong, numinous spirituality.

The School Sisters of Notre Dame taught grade school; there, we learned—"or else"—as we sat up straight in old wooden desks on runners. Discipline was delivered with a mere look, or, occasionally, a flying eraser or time on one's knees at the front of the room. Under the nuns' stern eyes we learned to read; memorized the Baltimore Catechism, the seven virtues, the eight beatitudes, the seven sacraments, and the Ten Commandments; and studied addition, subtraction, times tables, grammar rules, spelling words, and how to diagram sentences until we could do it in our sleep. We were quizzed and tested in history, geography, and science. Yet when it came time for serious religious instruction, it was the monsignor, not a nun, who appeared to hold forth on sin and its consequences.

Meanwhile, it was well known in the Catholic families around town that Father Scott, a local Jesuit priest regarded as a scientific genius, was a pedophile. He could be seen on any given afternoon riding his bike and stopping to "visit" at random houses where little girls lived. He pulled us onto his lap as he sat in our living room, right in front of our parents, and proceeded to slide his shaking hand up our shirts and, with his mouth quivering and perspiration beading on his upper lip, kiss us with an open mouth on the face and neck. It was as if the adults were blind to what Father Scott was doing; perhaps they couldn't imagine a priest was a pervert, or they were simply paralyzed by the authority of the Catholic Church. Regardless, this abuse went on for years, unchallenged and unreported, as he moved on to different families with little girls. We girls tried to defend ourselves by being vigilant and staying out of his reach. When we saw him pull his bike up in front of our house, or even riding nearby, my sister Bridget and I ran upstairs and hid in the back of our mother's closet until we knew he was gone. But in the adults' eyes, Jesuits—"jebbies," as my dad called them—were unimpeachable, the best of the best, real scholars and role models.

One evening at the dinner table, my eldest brother, then my idol, reported on his first day at Campion Jesuit High School. For the occasion, Tim was prominently seated to the right of our father, who sat at the head of the table. I had meticulously set the table to preempt my dad's looking around and finding the salt or pepper or bread or butter missing. At ten years old, I wanted everything to be perfect. And I was dying to be given the inside scoop on the high school academic adventure, one I was sure awaited me as well at St. Mary's Academy—the girls equivalent, I believed, to Campion.

Tim announced that the priests—the teachers now—had instructed the boys to "first of all, forget everything Sister Mary Kerosene ever taught you."

The knowing laughter and ridicule that my father and brother shared over this statement—a snickering insult that denigrated the nuns by ridiculing their church-given names—hit me right in the gut. I realized that I was not going to be included, ever, as an equal. All the teaching about the saints and sisters was a trick, a ruse, to get us girls to embrace our lesser status. We were presumed to be too dim to object. To be female was to be an outsider. So inconsequential were we that it never occurred to me, or them, that I might speak up and challenge them. The women who had dedicated their lives to teaching millions of Catholic kids around the world, whom we were taught to idolize, whose self-abnegation included giving up their names and assuming weird-sounding saint's names, were being openly ridiculed by a fourteen-year-old boy at the behest of the men of the Church. Without knowing how I might do it, I knew in that moment that I would have to fight to survive this place where a mere boy was taught that he was superior to a college-educated woman who had dedicated her life to the Church and the education of Catholic children.

The betrayal and ridicule of that exchange between my dad and my eldest brother settled deep inside of me as I sat with the family around that long oval oak table under the uneven glare of the five-bulb brass chandelier. Just like the fried eggplant I hated and had stealthily slid onto a deeply hidden ledge under the table, I refused to swallow the misogyny I was witnessing. I would slip through their clutches by modeling the perfect Catholic girl, excelling at academics, piano, speech, math, and any and all competitions in which I was allowed, and earning money as a babysitter and a grossly underpaid nurses' aide. I would play the cards I was dealt and covertly construct a life as an independent female in a male-dominated world, somehow. I would have to play by their rules, but as the late Texas governor Ann Richards, channeling the dancer Ginger Rogers, said, I would have to do it "backward and in high heels."

*   *   *

5

Even knowing that men ridiculed them behind their backs, the life of a nun, as far as I could see, was a good one—freer and happier than that of a married woman, certainly. I had many occasions to do surveillance on those nuns when I was sent with an empty basket from St. John's grade school to St. Mary's Academy's kitchen, just a few blocks away, to "get the lunch" prepared there for the nuns at our grade school. That kitchen always smelled wonderful, and it was filled with laughter and joking among the nuns working there.

I got an even better chance to imagine living the life of a nun one weekend when my sister Bridget and I stayed with a family friend who was a Dominican nun at a convent in River Forest, Illinois. Every night there were movies and popcorn and, again, lilting laughter. Some of the older nuns sipped sherry in the evening, just like my elderly never-married aunts. And they all took turns playing with a jumping toy grasshopper one of them bought for us, which they named "Hephzibah." Books were everywhere, and the place felt warm and homey.

At St. Mary's Academy High School, I took it all in as Sister Mary Linus, our principal, appeared to manage the men of the Church without their even realizing it.

The Monday following our spring dance my junior year, Sister Linus invited me into her office for one of our many chats. She proceeded to tell me, with a chuckle, that on the evening of our dance, Father Roger Lucey, one of the younger priests, had insisted she post chaperones in the stairwell. She said she had humored him, saying, "If it will make you happy, Father, I will sit right here with my book." She seemed amused by Father Lucey's paranoia about teenage sexuality, and said that she hadn't pointed out to him that this was her, not his, turf; she'd just let him think that he had won.

Unbeknownst to Sister Linus, that same priest had assaulted me the preceding year. I had just turned sixteen, and

Father Lucey had come to our front door when my parents weren't home and asked me if I wanted to drive his father's black Cadillac, which he had parked out in front. Of course I did! I had just gotten my driver's permit. We drove around for a while, and then he told me to pull the car into his father's driveway, which was across the street from my house and down a hill through a heavily wooded hospital yard. I was frightened (of what, I didn't know) so I scooted up the hill toward my house through the woods a few steps ahead of him. Suddenly, he grabbed me from behind with both hands tight around my waist. I couldn't understand what he was doing or why, but I was so scared I could hardly breathe. He laughed as I managed to wrench myself away and ran on ahead, blaming myself, wondering what I had done to make him do that.

I had been taught to believe priests were Christ-like and could do no wrong, even when their touch nauseated me. It had to be my fault. I ran away to my house, and he followed me right to the door, where my parents welcomed him in like a visiting dignitary, as they always welcomed the priests. Feeling physically ill and dirty, I went upstairs to my room and threw myself down on my bed. Downstairs I could hear him laughing and joking with my dad.

I had told no one about the priest's abuse, not even Sister Linus, whom I trusted more than anyone in the world. It didn't even dawn on me that I should. But looking back now, I believe she was onto him and his unholy interest in me.

On the night of the dance as I slow danced with my boyfriend, Tom (leaving the required "room for the Holy Ghost" between us), Father Lucey charged onto the dance floor, placed his hand on Tom's shoulder, and through gritted teeth ordered him, "Go back to Campion immediately." Campion, the old and renowned Jesuit boys' boarding school that my father had attended many years before, was about a mile away. As everyone else on the floor stopped and stared, Tom started out of the gym.

After shaking off my initial mortification, I decided to go with him right in front of Father Lucey and his sidekick, Father Burke, openly dismissing their authority. *You can't tell me what to do*, I thought, *and I will walk wherever I want with whomever I want. This is my school, not yours.*

Tom and I walked out of the gym and across the campus together. As we continued hand in hand down a very dark Beaumont Road toward Campion, we heard footsteps rapidly coming up behind us, so we crossed to the other side of the street. The sound of footsteps followed and got louder and closer, and then Father Burke stepped in front of us, blocking our path. He grabbed Tom by the arm and said, "You're coming with me."

Father Burke quickly led Tom away toward Campion, leaving me alone in the dark with the man who had assaulted me in a similar dark and isolated setting a year earlier.

Father Lucey put his arm around my shoulders and said, "And you are coming back with me."

At first I froze. Then I became determined to let him know he had no control over me, although I don't think I believed that myself. But I knew I had to get beyond his reach, and fast. I looked around and realized we were standing almost in front of my girlfriend Teddy's house, a Frank Lloyd Wright with three broad stairs leading from the covered driveway on the side of the house up to a wide stone-pillared porch and a front door I knew was never locked.

Determined not to let this loathsome priest see my fear, I pulled away from him and said, "I'm staying here tonight, Father," as believably as I could, and dashed down the driveway, up the few stairs, and into the house, slamming both the screen door and the heavy wooden door behind me. Then I locked the door and waited for Teddy to come home from the dance. No one else seemed to be home.

On that Monday after the spring dance, when Sister Linus invited me into her office, she had much more to share with me than she normally did during our chats, and she took her time.

"Peggy, Father Lucey called me yesterday to tell me he had something serious he needed to tell me about you."

My jaw must have dropped, because she quickly said, "Don't worry. I told Father Lucey, 'I know that girl. Don't try to tell me anything about her.'"

As I started to tell her what had happened at the dance and afterwards, she stopped me and said, "You don't need to tell me, Peggy."

*My God, Sister Linus knows about him and his interest in me*, I realized, although I didn't say anything more or ever tell her what had happened. As she said, I didn't have to. It was as if whatever had happened was just detail—small stuff I could get lost in—and she wanted me to focus on the big picture instead. She was teaching me how to handle the men of the Church.

The word "stalking," now a recognized legal offense, was then unknown to me, but I now know that this man stalked me throughout my high school years. Father Lucey popped up frequently in various places where I happened to be, from the bowling alley where we kids sometimes hung out to the hospital where I worked as a nurses' aide, once walking up behind me and remarking with a laugh, "Nurses' uniforms aren't supposed to be so modest."

I saw Sister Linus perform her Aikido-like moves on the priests repeatedly over the years, demonstrating the power of her silent strategy of appearing to accept their authoritarian moves and then neutralizing them. I could see that they had no real control over her, and decided they would have none over me either. With her guidance, I quit the Campion cheerleading squad, which featured five girls from St. Mary's Academy—selected by the priests—after two years.

When I tried out for the squad, I had no idea what I was getting into. It just seemed like fun. I was athletic and loved to do my version of a tumbling routine. But it was weird from the start. On several occasions, pictures of me spread-eagle in the air in the middle of a cheer or in some other uninhibited posture—taken by the boys on the school magazine and approved by the priests supervising them—were published in the magazine with suggestive captions like "*Agile Maggie Garrity stimulates student body with her rousing antics.*" After one photo of me and Tom, captioned "*Tom Harrington has things well in hand,*" appeared on the cover of the magazine, Sister Linus inquired of me, "Peggy, do you really need this?"—and for the first time it occurred to me that my involvement with Campion was neither the innocent activity I thought it was nor in my best interests. I was being used.

"Freedom is so important in life," Sister Linus told me more than once—a sentiment that might seem, on its face at least, at odds with the very notion of being a nun. But Sister Linus was pursuing freedom in her own way, and was modeling it for us. She led her order for a time, unbowed by the institutional misogyny, and forged a life of courage and integrity within the Church. This took some imagination. And guts.

*   *   *

My world in the 1950s and '60s was far removed from the idyllic television households of *Leave it to Beaver* and *Father Knows Best*. My mother could be found most winter afternoons on the "davenport" in the living room for hours, shades drawn, a newspaper over her face. Nowadays that would be diagnosed as clinical depression. Then it was "napping." Wisconsin winters lasted about nine months running, by my count, and it seemed she napped all winter, like a bear. She awoke like one, too.

My mother was happy on one afternoon each week: Wednesday, when she had her black hair and long red nails done by a tall, double-negative-spewing (e.g., "I didn't have no more ammunition") redhead named Danella, known more for her deer-hunting prowess than her salon skills. There was something to a woman having her hair done, it seemed. Mom was predictably happy only on those days at the "beauty parlor," where she read movie magazines under the dryer and chatted and laughed with dead-eye Danella.

On those days, I'd pedal my blue bike the four blocks to downtown to try to catch Mom toward the end of her appointment, when she was in the salon, happy. She would sometimes give me money to get an ice cream at the nearby drugstore, and I would sprint with my ice cream sandwich back up the stairs to meet her. Then I'd ride my bike alongside her as she walked home, trying to think of things to talk about that would interest her. I would have done almost anything to make my mother happy, to keep her increasingly dark moods at bay. The best moments of my childhood have her with a smile at the center. But those smiles wouldn't last. No matter how many races I won or A's I achieved.

In my family, it was understood that God had given me gifts and expected a return on his investment. My performance was expected to be superior; so when I got straight A's or won an athletic or academic competition, I was just breaking even. At my very first speed-skating competition—not more than seven years old, weighted down with heavy coat and snow pants like the near-sighted kid in *A Christmas Story*, blades on my hand-me-down black hockey skates scraping madly on the bumpy ice of the frozen Mississippi River—I propelled my body to the finish line past the other girls, then tried desperately to stop exactly at the finish line without breaking the tape, because I thought to win I had to get there first but not go a step farther. But I couldn't stop, and I went flying through the yellow tape, certain I had blown it. I was astounded and relieved when I was told I had won first place and was given the blue ribbon.

It would have taken much more than a blue ribbon to make my mother happy, though; I could tell that even then. Looking back, it's clear to me that she was overwhelmed and disappointed by her life in that small town. But I thought it had something to do with me.

In my house, dirty clothes were tossed over the upstairs banister and piled all the way to the first landing on the back stairs. We used to jump from the top of the stairs down into the clothes as sport, and we never got hurt . . . except when we were caught doing it. As we got older and Mom got more depressed, we kids were pretty much on our own, the older five of us roaming the big old Victorian house in small gangs as we fought for turf through hand-to-hand combat with clothes hangers and wadded-up dishtowels.

We were required to go to Confession and admit to infractions weekly, but no one dared confess or snitch to a parent on organized sibling crime, such as putting each other in the clothes dryer and turning it on, rolling each other down the several flights of stairs in a hamper, holding each other by the ankles over the upstairs banister railing and threatening to "drop you," or even dropping a hammer on a sister's head from high atop a tree house. My piano practice on the old chipped clunker in the front hall was a hazardous activity, as shoes and spit routinely landed on my hands as I played. Our family was set up the way Catholics were supposed to be—outwardly modeling the idea of a big, happy family—and for the most part we were happy. Mom seemed especially happy in the first few weeks after she came home from a week in the hospital with a new baby. Things were not always so happy, however, and they got worse as the years went by.

My dad and mom fought, increasingly, over his drinking, and our dinner hour became unpredictable and dependent upon when Dad chose to leave whatever bar he was visiting that day. Sundays were the worst. I always took my mother's side, all the while determined that there was no way I was going to get trapped in a life like hers.

We kids had hard evidence that Mom had once been happy. That it was possible. Photos of her from those days showed a vibrant, beaming and beautiful woman, dressed in finely tailored suits and dresses in the style of the day. She wore a gardenia over her right ear, holding for a moment her thick, shoulder-length black hair. In the most intriguing of them she was alone on a sandy beach, barefoot, wearing khaki shorts and a long-sleeved white blouse with a Peter Pan collar and, of course, the gardenia. She was gazing at the spot a few feet away where she had written "I LOVE BOB" in the sand with a stick she still had in her lap. Looking at the photo, I recalled her telling us she'd gone to Clearwater, Florida, to work during the war. I struggled to reconcile the depressed woman in front of me with a young woman hopping a train, leaving Minnesota for the first time, and heading for Florida to work in a dentist's office.

In other pictures, a beautiful and happy baby sat smiling on a blanket beside Mom in the grass of what appeared to be a backyard. In yet others she was dressed in heels and elegant suits, silk blouses with shoulder pads, sometimes wearing a hat with a face net and gloves. If there were background music, it would have been the big band wartime favorite "Sentimental Journey." There was not one in which she wore anything that said, "I'm a stay-at-home mom."

She used to tell us, cryptically, that the rules were different during "The War." If her smiling pictures were allowed to tell the story, one would think she'd actually preferred a world war to being at home with kids. But when the war ended, my father had returned and Mom's duty as a Catholic mother had been set. The closest she would ever again get to practicing her profession as a dental hygienist would be ordering her ten kids to brush their teeth. Between 1943 and 1950, she had five children.

\* \* \*

Born in 1947, the third child in a brood that would grow to ten, I grew up in the hysterical Wisconsin of Senator Joe McCarthy, who ranted into the living room from the same television set that announced *Father Knows Best*. On our knobby knees at daily Mass before the school day began, we prayed for the pope (who was supposedly infallible), as well as Russia (which wanted to blow us to smithereens). I got the message that even though "Father knew best," the whole world was pretty precarious and could come crashing down at any moment. But the perfect mother—on television, at least—would take even nuclear annihilation with equanimity, and always be perfectly dressed and coiffed.

My mother's life was, of course, nothing like that. She rarely dressed up. Seemed to have little fun. As I sat on the floor with my siblings watching the family comedies, I realized I didn't want to be like the television mothers either. They seemed just as trapped as Mom. There just had to be more out there for me.

Perhaps I would find it in the real job I was expected to land as soon as I turned sixteen. Realizing that a place to go in the afternoons and a paycheck would offer respite from my mother's world, I eagerly dove into the job hunt. As long as I got a job doing something my dad considered more respectable than being a waitress (there went my hopes of becoming a cool car hop at the A&W), I was free to do what I liked.

From sophomore year until high school graduation, I worked as a nurses' aide at Memorial Hospital, dodging the sexually predatory hospital administrator while earning 75 cents per hour to pay for my tuition and uniforms at St. Mary's Academy. I loved the job from the first day. It was there I began thinking I might really be able to become a doctor. My Uncle Mike, my dad's younger brother, was on staff at the hospital, and he taught me about medicine up close, allowing me to observe in surgery, labor and delivery, and the emergency room, where he explained everything that was going on.

Like my mother, I loved babies, and the newborn nursery was my favorite assignment. On many days, especially when the hospital was short- staffed, I had the bulk of the responsibility for bathing, changing, and feeding the babies, taking them to their mothers for nursing, and taking care of the mothers as well. The busier I was, the more I liked it. Dr. Mike suggested I could have a great future as a professional, doing the important work of a doctor. Maybe I could combine it with becoming a nun, I thought, which would make it more acceptable.

When I told my parents, my dad's response—"A woman is no damn good as a doctor"—left me speechless. I felt as if I had been punched in the gut. Dad wasn't a mean man. On the contrary, he was considered throughout the town to be kind and generous. He wasn't trying to be cruel. He just believed, as most others did at that time, that women were of less value professionally than men.

My dad's sexist remarks wounded me deeply and frequently, and if I complained he laughed it off. He told the world he was proud of me.

When it came time for college applications, my dad forbade my going to any college other than a Catholic women's college in the Midwest, even while making it clear I would have to pay for it myself. But when I went off to college, he didn't even inquire about what courses I was taking. Mom, on the other hand, secretly pushed me to major in something other than what she considered ordinary courses for girls. She urged me to major in chemistry when she learned that it was considered a good undergraduate preparation for medical school. Similarly, my Aunt Marg—my dad's never-married older sister and my mother's compatriot in subversion when it came to my future—pushed me on the sly to write to Bryn Mawr for an application. It was clear to me that whatever I might pursue I would have to go for under the radar and find a way to finance on my own. I was undaunted. I would find a way to become a doctor. Nuns, I could see, were committed to advanced education and to hospital work, and some were doctors.

In bed at night, as the house gently rocked with the 2 A.M. Minneapolis-to-Chicago train passing by a few blocks away, I would imagine myself dressed up in gloves, heels, and a stunning wide-brimmed felt hat with a feather on the side, like my tall, elegant, and educated Aunt Marg, and on the way to the city to glamorous work, maybe even as a doctor. Family lore was that as a young woman, Marg (after whom I was named Margaret Mary at baptism) had accepted a job as a translator for some governmental official in Mexico or Puerto Rico, and had gotten as far as Chicago with her newly purchased professional wardrobe before my grandfather called her back, saying he "needed her at home." Marg became a high school

Spanish teacher and vice principal instead of an international translator.

I promised myself I would never allow for that kind of male interference. I would wield the power in my life. And it was looking more and more like the convent was my best route to becoming a doctor and having a career.

## • CHAPTER 2 •


# CHICAGO BECOMES

# MY KIND OF TOWN


As it turned out, Sister Linus was the one who sent me out into the world and away from the convent. I went to her after receiving notice that I had won a scholarship to Rosary College in Chicago.

"This is a problem," I said. "What do I do?"

As if she had read my mind, she smiled and said, "It isn't a problem. Take the scholarship. Just because you have nuns in the family doesn't mean you should become one." Then, shaking her head, she assured me: "Peggy, go to college. If you still want us, we will be here when you finish." I trusted her counsel. This remarkable woman, more than anyone else, encouraged me academically, making me believe I could do anything, telling me, "You have a great mind."

Sister Linus was keenly aware that there were several nuns on my dad's side of the family, and was personally familiar with

18

my crotchety great aunt, Sister Mary Loyola, who was an aging member of Sister Linus's order, the FSPA, and for whom I was named. Sister Linus was part of an activist younger group of nuns whom Sister Loyola and the older nuns targeted as "renegade nuns." Sister Linus was ready for me when I sought her advice, appearing to have expected it.

To my dad's delight, Rosary College in Chicago, a four-hour train ride from home, had offered me financial aid that included a scholarship for tuition, along with a job as a live-in for a family with six kids ten and under that would take care of my room and board. My duties included all the family ironing, which I did in the basement. John, the ten-year-old boy would holler down demands from upstairs—"Peggy, I need a blue shirt!" One day when he shouted, "Peggy, I need a towel," I yelled back, "Drip dry!" and then heard his mother laugh.

I stayed in that live-in job the first year, but after that I lived in the dorms during the school year and an apartment during the summer. I fell in love with the excitement of the city, especially riding Chicago's famous "El" (elevated train) to and from work every day in the summers. The city of Chicago soon felt like home.

That first summer, the summer of 1966, I was a city girl like Mom had once been. Pleasing her was still my *raison d'être*, so whatever I did I packaged for her. She had always loved glamour, as was evidenced by her World War II photos, and she now seemed to be reliving that excitement through me. She also loved winning, so I tried desperately to do that regularly, working summers as a college model and twice competing for the title of queen of Chicago's St. Patrick's Day parade. The grand prize was a trip for two to Ireland, and I wanted to give it to my parents. When I was chosen first runner-up, twice (my prize was a wrist watch), the whole family came to Chicago for the parade and camped out and partied at the Palmer House hotel.

Modeling and beauty competitions did not come naturally to me; my mother suggested both, and I could feel her excitement when I succeeded even in these small ways. I felt alive and purposeful when I was doing things she admired and wanted for me.

Almost every weekend during the summers, I would literally sprint from Carson Pirie Scott in "the loop," where I worked on the College Board, across the bridge over the Chicago River to Union Station to catch the Friday night train home to Wisconsin. The first summer, on a lark, I scooted out at my lunch hour and traded in my ingénue flip for a stark geometrical haircut from Vidal Sassoon, determined to be part of the newest fashion craze. Wanting to bring whatever was new and different home to share, that weekend I took it upon myself to give my three little sisters my untrained version of the Sassoon cut. Each one happily hopped into the chair I placed in the yard, where I went to work bringing big-city Chicago to small-town Prairie du Chien.

I was ready to transform into a city girl. Excitement of any kind beckoned me, even when I didn't recognize the risks. Each adventure in the city made me want more. I wanted to be involved in everything, to experience the cultural scenes of art and music, including Rush Street, the museums, the Grant Park events, and the Ravinia concerts for which the city was famous. I was game for almost anything. So, in the summer of 1968, when Chicago was all about the Democratic National convention, I wanted to go, even though I had no real interest in politics.

Amid the street violence that summer, with a militarized Chicago police force chasing and beating Vietnam War protesters (among them a group later dubbed "the Chicago Seven" during their raucous criminal trial), the moment I was given the opportunity, I weaseled my way into what was fixing to become a historic event. Luckily for me, it started out at the Carson Pirie Scott department store, where I worked.

Big department stores like Carson Pirie Scott and Marshall Fields hired college girls every summer to sell and model college fashions. The girls were required to wear, daily, the designer outfit featured by each store. Pictures of the chosen girls and the names of their colleges were featured in a full-page promotion in the *Chicago Tribune*, as well as put on display in the stores' windows. These were status jobs and they could be very profitable: in addition to hourly wages, we were paid commission on everything we sold, and we were allowed to sell merchandise from any department throughout the store.

I quickly realized what this opportunity meant. Once I got a customer buying college clothes, I raced around the store with them to buy up purses, belts, coats, formal gowns, jewelry, and anything else I could think of, topping it all off with luggage to transport it. At the end of each week, the top College Board salesgirl was allowed to choose any outfit anywhere in the store for herself. I won that spot almost every week. Contrary to what the executives expected, but totally within the rules (and presaging my career as a lawyer) I used this opportunity to maximum benefit, and built up a wardrobe that went far beyond the typical college girl's fantasies. To the horror of the managers in the various departments I targeted, I chose fabulous knit dresses with matching coats, fur-trimmed coats and hats, and many other goodies that I would enjoy for years to come.

My work there also brought me into contact with many interesting visitors to Chicago, including a young woman who used her press pass for the Democratic Convention as identification when she paid for her purchases with a check. I told her I would give anything to get into the convention, and only half-jokingly asked her if she could get me in. To my delight, she invited me to go with her to her press office, a small paper run by her father located a few blocks away, to see if she could get me a pass. Her father said no, so I headed back to my train stop to go home.

I was hot-footing it down Michigan Avenue after work past bumper-to-bumper traffic, looking like some kind of confection in my Carson Pirie Scott uniform of grey patent leather heels, short grey-and-white plaid skirt, suede vest, and white high-necked blouse tied with a big white bow, when a delegate wearing a Michigan pass called out his limousine window, "How about dinner?"

Having learned to joust and parry with libidinous Shriners and other conventioneers during my summers working in downtown Chicago, I flippantly responded, "How about the convention?"

He startled me by firing back, "Sure." The guardian angel on my shoulder remained silent during this transaction, as she did at other odd times.

After some negotiations from his slowly moving limo, the Michigan delegate made me a deal: He would arrange the use of someone else's delegate pass to get me into the convention. But first I'd have to join him for dinner.

In a red booth in a dimly lit Italian restaurant full of delegates, waiters in white dinner jackets served us massive steaks, the standard midwestern luxury dinner, and then we were taken by limo to the Convention Center. I was detained in the guard station while my date went in to get my pass. The guards asked me for the delegate's name; I had already forgotten it, but they were, blessedly, distracted by Aretha Franklin's flubbing the lyrics of the national anthem on the radio.

"You blew it, baby," one of them said, laughing.

I held my breath until it was clear he was referring to Aretha and not me.

After what seemed like hours, my date finally returned with the pass and we headed into the convention and joined the Michigan delegation, where no one seemed to notice or care that there was a new player in their midst. When he told me to, I raised my hand in the caucus that made the historic vote to seat black Georgia delegate Julian Bond's alternate delegation. This was a huge news story, as was all the wild street activity, so television cameras and reporters were everywhere. We were standing near the back of the caucus room, and when the locked doors were opened I was the first one out, trying to avoid questions I knew I couldn't answer. As I ducked out into the hallway, I was blinded, and blocked, by waiting television cameras and reporters.

My off-and-on-again boyfriend, Gary, an Air Force Academy graduate in pilot training in Texas, couldn't believe what he was seeing when I appeared on his television. "Was that you last night?" he asked the next day when he phoned. I told him it was but didn't tell him the rest of the story, including how I had gotten in and what had happened at the end of the evening.

Our limousine driver took us back to the hotel where the delegation was staying, where we were supposedly going to join a party. Once there, however, I found myself in a conspicuously empty suite with no evidence of a party. When I surmised what was afoot, I leapt up and sprinted down the hall and to the lobby, Cinderella-like, leaving behind my brand-new London Fog trench coat, only to be reminded at the front desk that there were no cabs operating in the city that night. I phoned my roommate, Cheryl, a worldly flight attendant, who picked up the alarm in my voice and jumped in her car to rescue me.

As we drove back to our little apartment, I remember being taken aback by the sight of military tanks. Previously, I had only seen these ominous-looking vehicles on television reports from Vietnam. But now they had been in the streets virtually full time since the April assassination of Martin Luther King, Jr. and the June assassination of Bobby Kennedy. The city of Chicago had become an armed camp. Assassination had suddenly become a part of our political landscape.

Although I actually got to vote in the caucus and on the floor at the Democratic National Convention, it wasn't political on my part—just another irresistible opportunity to be in the action. I wanted to be where important things were happening. But a seed had been planted during my little urban adventure, even though I had only come for the party.

Later that evening I learned from the TV news that while I had been gallivanting about, peaceful protesters, including college kids as well as working reporters, had been brutally beaten with nightsticks after being driven against downtown buildings by police lines moving in a huge wedge. The raw show of police power during that summer, previously unknown to me, changed the way I viewed the world. Action was starting to mean much more to me than just having fun. And the full meaning of this moment in history might have eluded me if not for my naïve small-town girl pursuit of adventure in the big city.

Civil rights and anti-war marches were merging and creating a new social force that spoke to me. For the first time, I started to consider becoming a lawyer instead of a doctor.

\*    \*    \*

At the end of that summer, just before starting my senior year, I fell head over heels in love. I had remained religiously ignorant about contraception throughout college, and my thoughts of becoming a nun were not yet completely extinguished—but in early February of 1969, I found myself pregnant. That eliminated the convent as a career choice, and with it, perhaps, becoming a doctor. With no financial or moral support from my family, I had seen the convent as my one way to get to medical school and do something meaningful in the world. I was terrified and in disbelief that I was pregnant. I would have to get married now. I wondered how I could turn this challenge into an opportunity—something my dad used to preach, though he certainly hadn't had this circumstance in mind.

When Ron, always up for a gamble, proposed that we get married and move to California, I brightened up, and the wheels of my imagination roared into action. *Why not at least go for the adventure? We can always come back. We'll tell our families we'll return in a few years so they won't be too upset.*

In the meantime, I thought, this might at least give me a shot at going to medical, law, or graduate school. Leaving meant escaping what felt like the stranglehold of our families. Who knew what was possible in California; maybe everything. As a kid, all the pictures of it that I had seen had made the whole place seem like Disneyland. I had often fantasized about living in California while enduring the winter cold and summer humidity of the Midwest.

For the next few months until graduation, however, I would have to suffer through morning sickness and a desperate need to nap in the afternoon, all the while acting as if nothing was out of the ordinary and wearing dresses that would hide my pregnancy. I was finishing my senior year at the very proper Rosary College, after all.

That month our family gathered in Minneapolis for my brother Dan's wedding. Unbeknownst to me, Dan and his bride were also expecting a baby. As my mom, then forty-seven and the mother of ten, stood there holding my ten-month-old brother, Brendan, on her hip, I extended my hand to show her my engagement ring. She stared, crestfallen, at my hand, shifting the baby on her hip, and whispered, "What is that? Why now?"

"Why do you think?" I answered.

Then my dad walked over and, seeing the ring, cheered my impending matrimony with, "We'll have a big tent wedding in the yard this summer."

"We want to do it sooner," I said.

A few minutes later, throwing off her earlier look of defeat, my mom took me aside and said, like a drowning woman grabbing onto a lifeline, "You convert Ron. I will handle your father."

Seeming to immediately understand my predicament, my mother shifted into gear as my ally in what seemed like our secret girls' club, even as she saw all her dreams for me drifting away. She didn't know yet that I hadn't given up on them, but she soon would.

That spring, I took the LSAT and the MCAT, along with the chemistry graduate record examinations required for graduation as a chemistry major. I didn't know any women, let alone women with kids, who had a profession, but I was determined. Many of my classmates had come back from senior year Christmas break flaunting diamond engagement rings and romantic summer wedding plans. Not me. I had bigger plans.

Still, I was the first one down the aisle.

On a snowy and cold but sunny day in March 1969, in the tiny old chapel of St. Mary's Academy across the street from my parents' home, I married Ron, the father of my child. I gained Catholic bonus points by converting him to Catholicism, as my mother had instructed. The fabulous Franciscan nuns, whose star feminist and my great inspiration, Sister Linus, would later take on the Vatican over its treatment of religious women, helped put on my wedding. The statues of Mary, Joseph, and the other Catholic saints were covered in purple for Lent. I wore my sister-in-law Mary Kay's Priscilla of Boston antique lace gown, but with flowers in my hair instead of the veil, something I considered a feminist gesture. The day before the wedding Mass, I also personally installed new green shag carpet in the one bathroom of my parents' home. Then I set about making the potato salad to be served at the little reception in the convent dining room. I was back at school, with a new last name, on Monday.

\*　　\*　　\*

After graduation, Ron and I made our getaway to California, stepping onto a high wire without a net, on a virtual lark, with no job and no money. We escaped with all that either of us owned packed into Ron's gold 1968 Oldsmobile Cutlass. Although neither of us was an experienced camper, we needed to save money, so, for most of the next two weeks, we pitched a tent at night wherever we could. One morning we awoke to cows mooing nearby. In the dark we had unknowingly set up camp in someone's pasture. The herds of wild horses racing along the plains of New Mexico seemed to be headed in the same direction as our Cutlass.

The camping honeymoon continued until we hit the beach in Santa Monica on a magical night. The fragrance of the night-blooming jasmine poured in through the open windows as we drove into Santa Monica up the California Incline, the full moon lighting the sea beside us.

We found a furnished one-bedroom apartment on 12th Street in Santa Monica, in a building that didn't allow children but where that rule seemed easy to violate, and Erin was born a few months later, in October 1969. She and I hit the sunny streets and beach almost daily, baby bundled up in a blue plaid baby carriage with huge white wheels that I pushed up and down the same California Incline we'd driven in on. Christmas shopping in shorts and sandals that year prompted me to declare California home. Summer lasted all year, and with little rain. The place just seemed like an endless vacation resort, cool clothes and all. Blue or green lighting, discreetly hidden in the professional landscaping, spilled color on the sides of the apartment buildings during the nighttime hours. And the palm trees! To a Wisconsin girl raised in below-zero winters, this was the clincher. I loved the palm trees; they came with possibilities.

I applied for a job at a chemical company, but they refused to hire me because I had a baby at home. I bristled at the sex discrimination that continued to loom up to obstruct my path, from apartments that didn't allow kids to workplaces that wouldn't hire a woman chemist with a baby.

After a bit of research, I found out that I could go to law school at night, and immediately put in an application. I figured that I could attend classes three nights a week and be home with the baby all day. When I went for the interview, I was encouraged when the dean asked only for a college transcript and my LSAT score. It didn't matter that I had a baby. Now, everything seemed possible.

When my daughter was ten months old, I became part of the 10 percent of the first-year class that was female in night law school at Southwestern University. More than 50 percent of us would drop out before graduation. I wouldn't be one of them.

Maybe I wasn't going to be Mother Theresa. But I would be Atticus Finch.

# CHAPTER 3

# FROM NIGHT LAW SCHOOL

# TO PRESCHOOL

School provided balance in my life. Ron supported me then, both financially and emotionally, and seemed proud of what I was doing. Until he didn't come home to take care of the baby during final exams, that is.

This was the first of many unexplained disappearances. I knew Ron's family disapproved of my going to law school, so I thought perhaps he was doing his part to get me to drop out— but it wouldn't work. I felt so fortunate to be going to school that I didn't complain, even though I felt I was being sabotaged. I would just have to figure out all the logistics on my own without relying on him.

When I called the professor to ask if I could reschedule the exam I was missing because of Ron, the professor suggested he bring the exam to my apartment later that evening, "since your husband isn't there." I politely declined.

For the first year and a half of school, I hitched a ride to class from a guy who lived nearby, found through Southwestern Law School's ride-sharing program. He picked me up around 5 P.M. the three evenings we had school. Poor Paul. It got so Erin would stand on my briefcase and cry, "No Paul today, no cool today," when he came to the apartment door. I would hold her and explain as best I could where I was going and that I would be back soon.

Erin had me to herself all day every day and four out of seven nights, I told myself to assuage the guilt. It was very hard on both of us, but we also grew together. I took her to class a few times to let her see what I did, and she was particularly impressed by the catering truck that came at the break—even more so when Paul bought her a cupcake. She was mesmerized by the skeleton displayed by my torts professor, and later would ask me as I left for school if I was "going to see the bones."

Then, at the end of my first year of school, we found out I was expecting a second baby and needed to move out of our one-bedroom apartment to a house farther away. Ron surprised me one day with a little yellow Toyota Corolla that I ended up driving through the remaining years of school and for several years thereafter.

I loved both law school and having babies.

"You just want to keep them gasping," my mother said with her smile of approval when I got pregnant the third time. "And," she added, "you look like a *Harper's Bazaar* mother."

My male classmates were friendly and accepting, though they frequently asked, "Why are you going to law school?" and "Why does your husband let you go to law school?" My scripted answer to both questions was the non sequitur, "Because I can't play bridge." Bantering with these men was sporting, something that would also prepare me for the world of litigation I was about to dive into. Using skills honed surviving the child-grabbing priests of my childhood, I also adroitly outsmarted a couple of lecherous professors who seemed to view women students as freebie perks.

In a photo taken in front of the fountain outside the Dorothy Chandler Pavilion at my law school graduation in June 1975, I am holding two-year-old Bronwyn in her silk sailor dress. Her fat little baby hands rest possessively in my hair. Erin, age five, and Colin, age three, lean in close, squinting into the sun. I am in a black cap and gown. I can still feel the texture of the fabric of everything the kids are wearing. I can with all their baby pictures. Here the girls wear white patent leather Mary Janes with lacey top socks and satin bows in their hair—red for Bronwyn and pink for Erin, to match their dresses—and Colin is in a tiny sport jacket over blue shorts. All of them are holding on to me, and me to them. We are in this together.

Six months later, after I took and passed the California bar exam (which 50 percent of test takers failed), the scene was replayed when I was sworn in with hundreds of other newly minted California lawyers at the same venue. I had worked so hard, many nights without sleep, to create and care for a family and get my law degree and license. Now what?

My mother presented me with a beautifully wrapped red kidskin briefcase that Christmas. Her broad smile when she handed it to me seemed to say, "We did it! Now go do more and do it in style." When my dad joked that I would be "a lawyeress specializing in traffic tickets," my mother told me to ignore him. "And," she fired back at him, under cover of telling her own responsive joke, "you are a male chauvinist pig." I nearly fainted as my mother put my father on notice that he too could be the target of sexist ridicule. Mom had never been reticent to speak up, but something special was afoot. She started referring to him as "Archie Bunker," the caricatured sexist, racist, and ignorant patriarch of the hit television show *All In The Family*.

I could see that, along with my generation, Mom was getting fed up with misogynistic remarks defended as "just a joke," as if women didn't get it. She now seemed to be reading more than just movie magazines in her rare spare time. She openly admired Gloria Steinem and challenged my dad when he dismissed Betty Friedan, author of *The Feminine Mystique*, and Congresswoman Bella Abzug, and even Eleanor Roosevelt, as "women who look like that."

While she was proud of my accomplishment, Mom was hurt by my apparent desire to make California my permanent home. My twice-weekly phone calls home and frequent letters were no substitute. "You will come home for a month every Christmas," she said. That sounded good to me, since I didn't know what having a law license would mean. I agreed.

I had no illusions about having a future in a major law firm. I couldn't even type in 1975, had three little kids, had earned my law degree over five years of night school, and had no law firm experience. I felt lucky to be on the loose with my law license, thrill-seeker that I was. I just wanted to be in the game. From the get-go I hung out my shingle, eager to take on the world, especially the bullies. This was my opening to right the injustices I had been inventorying since childhood. I now had a platform. Besides, it was fun.

I wanted to get into court, so I happily took court appointments on criminal cases where the public defenders' office declared a conflict in a case involving two indigent defendants. That office could ethically take only one of those defendants, because a defense might include each one pointing a finger at the other, shifting the blame. This happened frequently. I had tried a few cases in Torrance while I was a law student in a clinical class, so I knew some of the judges there, and they assigned me the cases. I took anything that walked in the door, as well as anyone who was referred by indigent panels. I tried jury cases for as little as $300, and I couldn't believe I was getting paid to have so much fun. Money was secondary to the thrill, and would be for most of my career.

The only women lawyers I could track down were two go-getters who practiced family law, one in Beverly Hills and the other in the South Bay. These women warriors loved the court action that was a daily constant in the field of divorce and custody, and the two of them became the go-to lawyers in the field for divorcing women. That was the one field of practice in which women had any visibility. Women lawyers still made up only a small fraction of the bar, and it seemed women had to set up their own practices, as these two had, to receive recognition—but even then it was a hard fight to get there, as the field was still largely occupied by men. Both of these women generously took the time to take me to lunch and told me I would just have to work ten times harder than the men to be successful . . . but that they had done it and I could too. These insiders, without hesitation, acknowledged the sex discrimination in the profession that they both had worked around, under, over, and through. Yet they were both thriving in the law.

With them as inspiration, I rented an office and opened a solo practice. I got cards and stationery printed up, and bought a desk, a credenza, and two matching client chairs. I decorated my office with some pretty tiebacks that framed the floor-to-ceiling window, and a big ficus plant in a yellow pot. I followed my suitemates around like a puppy, learning everything I could.

Within the first few months, I tried and won my first criminal jury trial, a misdemeanor indecent exposure. The whole fee, start to finish, was $300. The guy was charged with lurking near a school, so my mother's antennae went up. For the first time I had to question whether I had a conflict with my client's best interests because of my own prejudices. Could I go home at night and look those three little kids of mine in the eye? Yes, I could. Any good trial lawyer should be able to represent any side of a criminal case. The Constitution guarantees everyone the right to a lawyer to defend himself. It was the burden of the prosecution to prove guilt beyond a reasonable doubt. My job as defense lawyer was to challenge the prosecution to do that. It was not to decide whether my client "did it."

I learned so much on that case, including the fact that double entendre would tumble from my mouth in a most perverse way whenever a case in any way involved sex. It got to the point that I could literally see the words floating across the courtroom as I tried hopelessly to grab them back. On the first day of trial I met Mr. Cummings at the elevator and asked him, "So, are you up for this?" He was speechless for the whole ride up to the third floor. Just the day before, one of the lawyers who gathered for lunch at the pub across the hall from our office asked me, "What do you think you can do for him? He sounds guilty as hell." My friend choked on his coffee when I responded, "I'm going to get him off." On this first occasion, it seemed a one-time stumble from too much time repressing dirty thoughts in Catholic school—but it turned out to be a proclivity that became more outrageous and pathological as I tried more cases, regardless of which side I represented.

Kids were my business plan, as it turned out. My compulsory one morning a week at the cooperative preschool Erin, Colin, and Bronwyn attended in Abalone Cove—a rundown cabana on the beach—morphed into a business development outing of sorts. Parents of other two- and three-year-olds, especially those sharing bathroom cleaning duty in a grubby old beach club, have a natural bonding that quickly leads to sharing all kinds of things going on in their lives, many of them with a legal spin.

We would continue to talk about our lives as we laid out the napkins, crackers, and juice on the four little tables for the kids' break, and as we watched over the construction of elaborate sand castles surrounded by saltwater moats. Many of us were renegades from colder climes, so our families were out of state. We talked about what we wanted for our kids if anything should happen to us. A number of parents hired me to do wills, and one sunny morning I was stunned to be consulted on handling a divorce for a young mom I took to be one of the most happily married among us. There we were talking family law over a picket fence as our little folk blissfully carried on with their shovels in the sand. These conversations created a sacred trust between us, and I put my all into making sure I delivered the best possible work for them.

No one works harder than a new lawyer except perhaps a new mother, and I was both. During these early years, as I tried to balance both roles in my own life, I would question my commitment to one of these roles whenever I felt overwhelmed by the other.

My guilt, I soon realized, affected my kids' perception of gender roles in the world of the 1970s. "Can't you be a just plain Mommy?" my daughter Erin asked one day. She was standing in the kitchen in her Indian Princess costume; I was in my last year of law school, and was working as an intern in the Torrance branch of the L.A. District Attorney's office. In those days, we were allowed to actually try misdemeanor cases even though we were not yet lawyers. I was sitting behind a pile of yellow legal pads and files that were spread all over the kitchen table, preparing for one of my first jury trials.

The question caught me right in the gut and confirmed my inner critic's judgment: I was a bad mother. *But wait a minute,*

I thought. *I'm putting in one morning per week at the preschool she and her two younger siblings attend. I make cupcakes and cookies for bake sales. Dammit, I keep them fed and dressed, even to the polished little white shoes and bows in the girls' hair to match their dresses.*

I also cut their hair myself, cleaned the house, ironed clothes, and washed the windows with vinegar and newspaper like good homemakers were supposed to do. I studied and followed Adelle Davis nutrition books and recipes to make sure we ate perfectly. No commercial television programs, except *The Waltons*. I even built a fence and sandbox with a cover to keep out the cats . . . while I was pregnant. I had gone to law school three nights a week, spreading a three-year curriculum over five so I would be home with them all day and most nights. But now, indicted by my sweet five-year-old, I could come to only one conclusion: I was a bad mother.

I went on like this, filled with angst and guilt, for months. Finally, I mustered the courage and asked Erin, "Honey, what do you mean?" Her response? "You know, like Laurie's mom." Her friend Laurie's mom was an RN! It seemed she associated nurses with femininity. In those days nurses wore starchy white hats and crisp uniforms. Would Erin accept my lawyering more if I wore a costume? I wondered. Say, like the black robes and wigs worn by barristers in the UK?

Dress-up was Erin's favorite play. At the preschool she headed straight for the playhouse and its racks and baskets full of flouncy dresses, old high heels, pearl necklaces, feathered boas, floppy hats, and sparkly purses. She ignored the cowboy getups and boy clothes, as well as the trucks, I offered her in an effort to balance out the cultural role-play I assumed limited little girls in our society. She put dolls around the little tables, pots and pans on the stove, and prepared play feasts while dressed to the nines.

She seemed spawned from the high-heeled, pearl-bedecked, crinoline-fluffed mothers from fifties family shows like *Lassie*, *Leave It To Beaver*, and *Father Knows Best*.

Then there were the observations of my son in 1976, shortly after I started practicing.

"Can boys be lawyers too?" four-year-old Colin asked me one day in 1976. We were in Torrance Superior Court, then a real boys' club, where I was one of very few female members of the bar. I was wearing a demure knit dress and high heels. Colin was dressed up, too, in little blue trousers and a white shirt under a checked vest. He was standing by my side, holding my hand.

*Huh?* I thought. *Where did that idea come from?* He couldn't imagine what men were doing in court. The judge was a man, the bailiff was a man, and most bizarre of all to him, the opposing lawyer was a man. I had to restrain myself from saying, "Obviously not… just listen to that guy." As Colin recalled it many years later in an essay published at NYU, I said, "Yes, if they study really hard and pass a test."

So, I thought with a smile, it is possible to turn people's biases upside down. This is encouraging. There are real possibilities for change in the world.

# PART TWO

# CHAPTER 4

# THE ASSASSIN AND ME

A year after I started practicing law, I got what would be the first of many high-profile cases. It involved would-be presidential assassin Sara Jane Moore, and it revealed me for the adrenaline junkie I was: yearning for action while ignoring the economics of my situation. In one of my first cases, I would actually lose money.

I was set with a legal pad and pen in my new red briefcase, which was sitting on the seat beside me. I was going to meet Sara Jane Moore. Sara Jane was serving a life sentence at Terminal Island Federal Prison in Los Angeles after being convicted of attempting to shoot President Gerald Ford in 1975 in front of San Francisco's St. Francis Hotel.

Sara Jane, who reportedly was not allowed to see her young son, Frederic, wanted "unspecified legal help." As a mom, I couldn't imagine the pain of life imprisonment away from my kids. On the other hand, I couldn't imagine taking a shot at anyone, either, let alone the president of the United States. One of the attorneys who sublet an office to me popped into my office one afternoon and told me she didn't want to get involved and asked me if I was interested. Boy was I! The action was centered in the courtroom, so I wanted more than anything to be there. In order to become a trial lawyer—in order to get into court—I would have to take chances. What better way than to grab on to a wild ride with an assassin? She had to be incredibly interesting, at the very least.

I had done criminal defense work in the state court, and with some success, even at this early stage of my career. I'd donned the spirit of the champion of the oppressed and fought hard for what I perceived as justice . . . catching cops in lies, and getting small-time criminals out on motions attacking bad police work. But this was different. Sara Jane Moore was a fascinating character, a middle-aged woman who had tried to kill the president. I wanted to talk to her and see what made her tick. Was she a monster? The press reports made her sound like a menopausal madwoman with too much time on her hands. Would the notorious prisoner be appalled at the child masquerading as a lawyer? Would I have a clue as to what to say to her? Would they even let me into the prison?

I didn't even know how to get to Terminal Island! Driving alone in my little Toyota, I pulled over just after getting over the Vincent Thomas Bridge to ask a man along the way, "How do I get to Terminal Island Prison?"

His response: "Don't pay your taxes."

I found my way onto the federal reservation and parked. I looked up at the palm trees swaying in the sunny breeze, the ocean, and then at the guard towers, where I saw guns. It was a display of raw power, but it didn't make me nervous in the slightest. After all, I had seen lots of guns growing up in Wisconsin, where everyone hunts and schools, businesses, government offices, and courts close for deer season in November.

I headed to the main gate, where I was required to go through the first metal detector of my career. The guard was friendly enough, and I would get to know him well over the next several months. I signed in at the desk, showed my bar card, and told them I was there to see Sara Jane Moore. A prison matron and a male warden dressed in business attire just smiled at me and laughed between them, perhaps at my earnestness and naïveté. Having grown up as a Catholic girl, I was used to seeing women looked at like that, and I wasn't going to allow it to get in the way of my adventure. In fact, being taken seriously by obvious authority would have surprised me. Besides, I reasoned, every moment at this point in my life felt like part of a reconnaissance mission.

The matron, with the authority of a mother superior, told me to have a seat. Obediently, I did. It was all oddly familiar. The waiting room felt like the lobby of the hospital I had worked in during high school, with comfortable chairs and decent lighting. The walls were freshly painted and the place was clean, likely scrubbed down by the honor prisoners. It reminded me of the way we Catholic school kids were lined up on our knees across the length of the classroom, armed with clumps of soapy steel wool, and moved across the floor in a line as we scrubbed the floors to a whole new color. We embraced the janitorial task with the pride of the oppressed because, unlike the "public school," Catholic schools didn't receive tax money, so we kids had to take care of the place ourselves. We made it just one more competitive game, trying to outdo each other using "elbow grease," as prescribed by the nuns.

Terminal Island didn't reek the way the county jail did, or like the courthouse lockup where prisoners were kept while waiting for their court appearances. I had spent lots of time in lockup at the courthouse and the jail, visiting the indigent criminal defendants I'd been appointed to by judges. Those places were rank with the smell of urine, sweat, and too many men with too little air in one place. The stench of those jails and holding cells had a metallic air.

With its green lawns and basketball courts, Terminal Island felt like a college campus, even down to the interview room we were given. I was reminded of the "fishbowls" at Rosary College where we received guests and could be observed by the nuns. After only a few minutes the warden, keys jangling like a character in a movie, came to get me and led me down the hall to an office-sized room with a desk and four chairs. He was pleasant as he showed me to mine and told me to wait. I thanked him. I was as painfully polite and deferential to the wardens as I had been to the nuns and priests during my sixteen years in Catholic school.

Windows along the wall facing the corridor made it clear that anyone in this room could be observed throughout our meeting. It appeared that when the door to the room was closed we would at least have privacy to talk—but there was little I could imagine Sara Jane might say to me that she hadn't already said in the various media interviews she had done. Thank God I was so naïve! It served me well in getting me through the visit. The trial lawyer's ego and swagger were as yet unknown to me.

A few minutes later, Sara Jane appeared, smiling and chatty. She had a high-pitched chirp and curly brown hair, and was wearing a work-type shirt and loose pants. She sat across from me. Though she had to keep her hands on the table the whole time, there was an air of self-confidence about her, as if she were hosting me for tea. In fact, she seemed amused by my youth and inexperience. Her blue eyes sparkled as she spoke in long, relentless stream-of-consciousness sentences. I couldn't get a word in, but that suited me just fine. I was thrilled to hear her speak— even if she didn't seem particularly interested in discussing her legal issues. I sat across the table from her staring and thinking, *Holy shit! A real assassin!*

She talked about her needlepoint, and even promised me a piece of her work . . . which she still owes me. *A needlepoint artist,* I thought. *A real woman.* I knew nothing about her background, other than that she had attempted to shoot President Gerald Ford. During our chat, however, I could tell that she was smart, educated, and cultured. This was not just a nutty, menopausal madwoman, as she had been made out to be in press accounts.

Without warning, Sara Jane veered into talk of the assassination attempt, blithely explaining, as she had to the press in interviews, that if Gerald Ford (who had not been elected) had died in office, Nelson Rockefeller (who was also not elected) would have become president, and the world would have seen that big money corporations were really running the country, which would start a revolution. In the breezy tone of a neighbor in a coffee klatch, she also offered what became something of a mantra: "There comes a point when the only way you can make a statement is to pick up a gun." I tried not to show my shock as I fought to keep my jaw in place. She had been quoted saying the same in a *Los Angeles Times* article on September 25, 1975, but I didn't know that at this point. I felt as if I didn't know anything about anything. The only thing I was sure of was that I couldn't let my ignorance show.

Sara Jane spoke to me of federal agents and policemen who arrested her by their first names, as if they were friends of hers. She spoke with the same familiarity about "Popeye" Jackson, George Jackson, and other "street radicals." I sat there, fascinated and stunned, as she bounced effortlessly from talking about needlepoint and classical music (she was an accomplished violinist) to wild political intrigue and more. I struggled to imagine this obviously well-bred woman hobnobbing with the black radical underground as well as cops. This woman whom the press had diagnosed as "crazy" struck me as shockingly sane. I was too naive to know who "Popeye" Jackson or George Jackson was (both black activists were murdered). In fact, I didn't know anything about the radical left organizations or prison movement in San Francisco with which Sara Jane had been involved. Neither did I know she had been spying, as a double agent, both on and for the FBI, San Francisco PD, and other police organizations, as well as the radicals.

The notion that an apolitical, sheltered Catholic schoolgirl, now an overbooked mother and new lawyer, was sitting in this room with a would-be presidential assassin was almost too much to believe. Sara Jane was yammering on about people and things that meant nothing to me. I didn't dare tell her how little I knew. I wanted more of the excitement. I left the prison that day not knowing what I could do for her, but certain there had to be something.

Blindly idealistic, and awestruck by my status as an officer of the court, it didn't dawn on me that this new attorney-client relationship could put me at any risk, professionally or personally. I also didn't know how consuming it would be, or how my life would change during its course. This game was being played in a real ballpark under the lights, not the vacant girls' league lot of my childhood. In exchange for getting to "play in the boys' league," I would fear nothing and go all out. I would give everything I had, and more.

I couldn't for the life of me see Sara Jane—or "Sally," as she called herself by the end of my first visit—carpooling and making lunches. She didn't talk about the cute things her son did. In fact, Frederic didn't seem real. Instead, Sara Jane was consumed with the cat-and-mouse institutional life of prison and its built-in rules—retribution, cell shakedowns, solitary confinement, and virtually constant conflict with authorities and other inmates. She thrived on the chaos. I was troubled that her son's custodial arrangements seemed to bother her mostly because she didn't like the people he was with. It was about her, not the young boy whose life had been upended because of her actions. She did not seem sad, and that seemed odd too. Then I checked myself: my own neighbors criticized me for practicing law while I had little kids at home with babysitters, seeing my actions as selfish. Maybe Sara Jane and I had more in common than I cared to admit. I found the excitement irresistible.

Sara Jane's restrictions in prison were severe, but she had managed to maintain contact with some interesting characters from the outside, and she asked me to be available to them. She was in communication with a priest, a freelance reporter, and lawyers for people I had never heard of. While I could understand that she wanted to maintain a connection with people beyond the prison walls, there was really no reason for me to become involved in this effort. The motion for a new trial was premised upon her not having had sufficient time and opportunity to consider the import of her pleading guilty to attempted assassination of the president, so I didn't need to know much of her background or political involvements. But I didn't know how to say "no" to clients at this point, so I agreed to talk to anyone she wanted me to, even going so far as having lunch with a few of them.

Looking back now, I am shocked at my cavalier behavior and the unnecessary risks I took. My work for Sara Jane was on a very narrow issue. I was making a motion that relied essentially on the court record and the opinion of an expert that Sara Jane had not entered her guilty plea knowingly and voluntarily, and that she had therefore been denied the right to due process.

At the time I don't even think I knew of Sara Jane's long history with the federal government, including service in the military years before as a WAC—and time as a patient in Walter Reed.

Three months before Sara Jane's September 1975 assassination attempt on President Ford, "Popeye" Jackson, rumored to be an FBI spy as well as the founder of United Prisoner Union, had been murdered, and some activists believed that Sara Jane was responsible for setting him up. She had become close to him while spying for the FBI.

My work for her did not involve trying to prove her innocence or putting up a defense against the charges for which she was convicted and sent to prison. I had tunnel vision as I set out to prove that she had been denied the right to due process and a trial. I don't know what I would have thought if I'd known what I learned later—that the only reason she didn't kill Ford was that the sight on the gun she used was off by six inches.

Likewise intriguing was the history of Sara Jane's gun ownership, especially the fact that she acquired the .38 Smith and Wesson she used from an unlicensed dealer who had bought it from an SFPD officer. She also happened to be helping ATF set that dealer up, and on September 21, 1975, the day before the assassination attempt, had accompanied agents of ATF, as well as SFPD, to his shop in Danville, according to *Taking Aim at the President*. So she wasn't just blowing smoke when she dropped all those names of good guys and bad guys. It was difficult to see who belonged to which group, and exactly what Sara Jane's role was, but I didn't need to know all that during the months I worked on her case. My goal was limited . . . thank God.

If there were federal agents assigned to investigate me back in 1977, when I was the young suburban mom driving a yellow Toyota, they must have thought they had the wrong file. They would not have found any sign of rebellion in my life. No protests or political involvement at all, besides weaseling my way into the Democratic Convention in '68. I had barely a passing acquaintance with the trial of the Chicago Seven, even though it sprang from the riots in Chicago during that same convention.

Yet here I was, representing a purported would-be presidential assassin.

As instructed by Sara Jane, I picked up the *Playboy* magazine interview she had done several months before after our first meeting. It was the first *Playboy* magazine I had ever seen. I was shocked that this supposed radical had given an interview to a magazine that depicts nude women in erotic positions. In the interview, "The Real Reason I Tried to Kill President Ford," which had caused a sensation, Sara Jane presented herself as a suburban housewife turned revolutionary. She had said much the same at the time she entered her guilty plea in open court.

I had no client control at all in those early days, especially of Sara Jane. Over the next several months, it became common for my eight-year-old daughter, Erin, to accept collect phone calls from prison and call out to me, "Mom, it's Sara Jane," while I was in the middle of poaching eggs or making oatmeal for my kids. Perhaps Sara Jane liked the contact with normal humanity, as she essentially joined us for breakfast for the next several months.

Several weeks after that first meeting with Sara Jane, I was summoned to the phone during Bronwyn's fourth birthday party at Farrell's ice cream parlor. Sara Jane had phoned my office with the news that the warden was not going to allow her to see me anymore unless she agreed in writing to submit to a strip search before and after each visit. My secretary kept her on one line and me on the other, going back and forth between us in a three-way conversation. Sara Jane was not going to submit, and she demanded I take legal action immediately. The Happy Birthday siren and bells were going off in the background.

"Okay," I said. "Tell her I will file something with the court." The reality of my involvement with this woman was starting to register. I had a client who insisted on running the show, from prison. This case was going to be all-consuming.

On the way home, my car full of kids and presents and balloons, I started to fret, wondering how I could manage an assassin and preschoolers in the same day. Both had tantrums when I didn't leap to meet their demands. Maybe there were more similarities than differences.

My planned visit to Sara Jane for the next day was aborted when she refused to submit to the strip search. That evening, with my babies in bed and husband at home, I headed to the office to do some research. I learned that I would have to get an order from the court to see my client. But it was tricky stuff. I was asking for a mandatory injunction against the federal government, and I had no idea what I was doing. I would have to go downtown the next day for further research at the federal library. I think I would have preferred to submit to the strip search myself.

While I was buried in books at the library, Sara Jane called my office and said she had gone on a hunger strike. A television network was coming out to the prison to interview her for the evening news. Somehow, the warden had already given his approval. This was in the days before cell phones, so I had to run out to the pay phone every hour or so to keep up with what was happening. I felt like Bronwyn's hamster, Stella, on a wheel that just never stopped. As Sara Jane's lawyer, I would have to be present when the press interviewed her. So I headed out to the prison.

When I arrived, I discovered that because Sara Jane had refused the strip search that was a condition of her meeting with me, I would be required to sit all the way across the room from her, while the producers and technicians brought out by the network, as well as anchor Christine Lund, were allowed to be right next to her, even touching her to attach microphones. I was nervous, though I don't know what I was worried about. She was already sentenced to life imprisonment. Still, it felt like watching a kid doing dangerous things on the playground monkey bars and knowing you won't be able to get to her in time to prevent her from cracking her head or running into the street.

There was an elaborate lighting setup, with piles of cords and cables all over the floor. Any number of things among all the equipment, handled by numerous technicians, could have served as a weapon, and yet no strip search was required of Sara Jane as a condition of the press visit. One might reasonably conclude that the authorities wanted Sara Jane to appear on the news, because they could certainly have prevented it. One could also conclude that since I wasn't being let near her, they did not want her meeting with me over legal issues. This was not reasonable, so I decided that I would have to get a court order for attorney visits with my client.

The next day, after an all-nighter preparing papers, I was off to San Francisco to visit the judge. I got my order, but the warden still would not let me in. It seemed a clear violation of the right to counsel, and also a direct violation of a court order.

So I had to regroup again. That night after the kids were in bed, I sat down at our kitchen table and perused my blue practice guide. I learned that the only remedy was to file a motion for an order finding someone in contempt of the judge's order; but whom should it name as the bad guy violating the order?

Oh, God: the warden, his boss (the head of the Bureau of Prisons), and their boss . . . the United States attorney general, Griffin Bell. I headed back to court, a Lilliputian tattletale in a world of giants. After giving my papers to the judge's secretary, a charming elderly woman who seemed to feel sorry for me.

I took a seat on the church-like bench in an otherwise empty courtroom, crossing and uncrossing my legs like I used to in second grade, half expecting to get cuffed by some nun for fidgeting. The elevation of the judge's bench in the federal courtroom, with the flags on the side and a huge seal of the United States of America looming behind it, made me feel even smaller.

I have always felt the awesome power of the law in federal courtrooms. There is no mistaking the importance of what is going on there. On this afternoon, I could hear Judge Sam Conti bellowing his displeasure to whoever was on the line at the US attorney's office. "Let her in, for Christ's sake. She's filing a contempt," I heard him say.

I was puzzled that it took a federal judge to stop them from interfering with my visits to my client. On the other hand, I was struck by the fact that a prisoner—even an accused would-be presidential assassin—whose rights were being trampled could get a federal court to take action. And through a rookie lawyer, no less. I was sure justice would prevail, the sentence, plea, and conviction would be thrown out, and Sara Jane would be granted a new trial on the assassination attempt. I didn't bother to think about the consequences of potentially winning the motion for a new trial.

The judge signed another order—this one consented to by the US attorney, in order to avoid a contempt hearing—that required the warden to let me in. My faith in the legal system, blind as it may have been, was given new life with this development.

It was too late to serve the order on the prison that night, but before going home, I met up with my lawyer chums in the pub next to our office and offered up my "war story," to which all listened raptly. I finally had something interesting to contribute. It gave me a sense of belonging.

*   *   *

My next visit to Terminal Island was truly strange, and everything a small-town girl could hope for. Sara Jane and I were put in the visitors' area in the yard, where we sat at picnic tables. I was dumbfounded when Sara Jane pointed out to me that the skinny girl sitting at a table across the way was "Squeaky" Fromme, one of the notorious "Manson girls." She, too, was in for trying to shoot Ford, just a few weeks before Sara Jane's attempt, also in San Francisco. I couldn't help wondering why two women would try to do that. Squeaky, tiny as she was, did indeed give me a chill with the way she looked at us. I was relieved when it was time for me to go home.

After several days of interviews, research, and kibitzing with other lawyers in the local pub, I decided that Sara Jane's guilty plea might be vulnerable to attack. I hopped a plane to San Francisco to talk to James Hewitt, the federal public defender who had represented her. I was delighted when Hewitt talked to me on the phone and agreed to sit down with me. I would get a copy of the court transcripts from Moore's plea hearings. But I really needed to know more than a transcript could tell me; I needed his take.

Hewitt was a fiftyish fellow who was something of a cowboy, and he seemed to revel in attention from a girl lawyer who zealously equated court to church. Maybe that was what helped me get access to him; in any event, he was most gracious and charming. He took me to lunch, where he kept me spellbound with his stories.

My almost formal respect for older men, I now realize, was a significant asset for me as a young lawyer. I noticed early on that I could get almost any of those established guys to talk to me if I just asked with a certain amount of awe in my voice. Trial lawyers cannot resist an audience.

Hewitt had been the first federal public defender in the country, when the office was first established. He pointed out that when he was handling the Moore case in court, F. Lee Bailey was going to trial on the infamous Patty Hearst case in the same courthouse. Ironically, Sara Jane had worked on the People In Need program established by the Hearsts as ransom for Patty while she was still held captive by the SLA. The two women, who had never met but whose lives intersected, had both been tried as criminals at the same time.

I am not sure whether Hewitt actually said it to me, or if I imagined that he did, but in my head I can still hear him saying that he was going "to blow F. Lee Bailey out of the saddle and show him how criminal defense is done." Bailey had presented a defense of brainwashing, which meant his client had to take the stand and testify. This had opened the door to cross-examination of this society girl turned radical and bank robber—not a good idea. We all know how that turned out. Patty Hearst, a kidnapping victim, was sentenced to prison for seven years.

It was a strange time in San Francisco. Numerous psychiatrists had been appointed by the court on both cases to evaluate the defendants. Both were found competent to stand trial. Hearst went to trial and jail. Sara Jane also pled guilty, and was now in jail with a life sentence. As I sat with Hewitt, who was truly gracious to me, I couldn't help think that the two women, both would-be assassins, had been represented by two powerful male lawyers caught up in their own duel.

Hewitt stunned me with his story of being forced to trial on Moore with less than thirty days to prepare. The government had spent the preceding two months examining Sara Jane to determine if she was sane to stand trial. With that schedule, no one would be sane, especially the lawyers. Sara Jane had suddenly decided to enter a guilty plea rather than be rushed to trial, and, though he'd objected on the record, Hewitt did not seem to have done much else to stop her. If she had done it only because of the pressure, I wondered, could it be that her plea was under duress and was not knowingly entered? Sara Jane had stated in open court at the time of her plea that she had not been coerced by anyone. But a guilty plea must meet a high standard of being knowing and intelligent to be an acceptable basis for conviction.

If Sara Jane's plea didn't meet those high standards, it would be very important to the motion. It would also take a hell of a lot of nerve for me, a rank amateur, to accuse Hewitt, a seasoned federal public defender—even if only indirectly—of ineffective assistance of counsel. Sara Jane had changed her plea from not guilty to guilty right before she was to go to trial and against her attorney's advice. She'd refused to participate in her own defense—which, Hewitt believed, should be based on diminished capacity. Sara Jane was not going to be cast as a crazy. She would rather go down as a dangerous radical.

Knowing how routinely I was able to get much lesser trials on crummy misdemeanors continued for months at a time, and repeatedly, I found the denial of a motion to continue a trial of this magnitude odd, to say the least. Even traffic code violations would be continued for months if a continuance of trial were requested.

I arranged for a prominent psychiatrist who had been head of the California Psychiatric Association to interview Sara Jane during a visit with me. She formed the opinion that Sara Jane's plea did not meet the legal standard—that it had not been made "knowingly and intelligently." This means she had to understand the consequences of waiving her right to trial and being sentenced to life in prison, and the psychiatrist believed that Sara Jane had not understood those consequences. It was not a consciousness of guilt that drove her to the plea. It was fear of looking like a "madwoman"—Hewitt's proposed defense.

Relying on that expert declaration, I filed a motion to set aside Sara Jane's guilty plea, arguing that her plea was not based upon information she possessed but rather on a *lack* of information. It hit the wire services, and almost immediately I received a phone call from a UPI reporter named Mary Neiswender, who happened to live just up the hill from me in Palos Verdes, beyond the locked Crest Road gate to Rolling Hills.

After we spoke on the phone several times, Mary invited me to meet with her at her house rather than at my office—because, she informed me, I was no doubt under surveillance. It did feel as if I was being followed a lot of the time, but it didn't really bother me, and I didn't feel in any kind of danger. Mary seemed unfazed by the possibility of being under surveillance and sort of laughed it off. I tried to emulate her bravado.

Mary seemed like a kindred spirit, and we hit it off right away. With a big smile and short curly brown hair that was sort of like Sara Jane's, she was a high-energy mother of two kids and had what looked like a normal home life. We spent many hours sitting around her kitchen table talking about anything and everything. She said she was writing a book about Sara Jane, and seemed to have a lot more information about her than I did.

Intuitively, I understood that if there was going to be press coverage of a case it was best to deal with it head-on when press pursued me. I found Mary witty and personable, and she had written a remarkably accurate piece on the motion I had filed, analyzing it as a "three-pronged attack" on the guilty plea. She was interesting, great fun, and a veteran of the courts from whom I could learn a lot. She seemed to know what she was talking about, and I knew she had traveled through some scary terrain in her crime reporting.

Mary was a fearless and tenacious veteran newspaper reporter at a time when women were just as much outsiders in her field as they were in mine. And she had been at it about ten years longer than I. Grisly murders, especially the Charles Manson family murders, were her specialty, but she was drawn to any good criminal story.

While Mary, Sara Jane, and I evolved from different life experiences, and might seem to have nothing in common, we were all adventure seekers, and we were crossing paths at a dramatic moment in history when women were not welcome in the newsroom, the courts, or the radical underground. I was the thrill-seeker lawyer pursuing justice, Mary was the gutsy reporter chasing a crime story to the gates of hell, and Sara Jane was a disaffected, middle-aged suburban wife and mother who wanted to be a revolutionary and became a would-be assassin.

When Mary asked to see the court transcripts I had gotten in San Francisco, I not only said yes but also agreed to bring them up the hill to her . . . like the carhop at a local A&W. I piled Erin, Colin, and Bronwyn into my car (this was in the days before mandatory kid car seats) and drove up Crest Road, which became a one-lane unpaved dirt road near the top, parked, got out, and walked in the dark to the locked chain link gate where Mary was waiting. As I handed the transcripts over to her and turned around to go back to my car, headlights coming up the hill toward me blinded me. Suddenly fearful of I didn't know what, I jumped into my car, turned it around, and sped past the other car and down the hill. Whoever it was scared me—deliberately, it seemed. Unnerved, I drove around the hills for a while instead of going straight home. Colin remarked as I zoomed down the hill, "Mom, you drive like 'Police Woman.'"

*He is not allowed to watch that show*, I thought.

\*     \*     \*

On a sunny and beautiful afternoon a week or so later, I was giving each kid a ride on my new moped. When Colin's turn came, I headed a little ways up the same hill, a not-much-traveled road. The blue Pacific sparkled below. Catalina Island jutted out of the blue, a sentry to the Santa Monica Bay and the shoreline from Palos Verdes to Malibu. Colin was unusually quiet, even somber, when he should have been shrieking with pleasure on the back of a "motorcycle." When I asked what was wrong, why he didn't seem to be having any fun with our new toy, he said, "I thought we were going to see Sara Jane and I was scared."

Puzzled—Terminal Island Prison was a long way in a different direction—I said, "Scared of Sara Jane? Why?"

"No, I'm not scared of Sara Jane," he said. "I'm scared of the men who chased us down the hill in the black car."

He sensed danger, and it caught me in the gut. What was I doing? How, and why, had I put that frightening event out of my mind? What kind of mother was I, really?

I remembered a recent visit with Sara Jane. We were in a visiting room, brightly lit and bare but for the table and our two chairs, under the watchful eye of several heavily armed guards. The air was decidedly different from my first visit. I was less welcome now than I had been before I filed the habeas motion. Sara Jane passed me a heavy manila envelope, whispering, "We had a cell shakedown this morning, and I have to get rid of something. Stay away from the metal detector on the way out." She wore what I considered a smug smile.

*Why is she saying that*, I wondered? *No one goes through the metal detector on the way out.*

Something—probably the voice of God—told me not to hand it back to her . . . and also not to ask her about it. I was starting to get uneasy with her, especially her demands, which went beyond normal lawyering. After that, she spent the next hour happily chatting away about prison intrigue. It felt as if we were the only lawyer-client duo in the room that day; the guards were entirely focused on us. I knew I was getting into risky territory, but I didn't know how to draw lines. Not with a woman like this.

I had already been snookered into forwarding a letter to her "husband," a black radical named "Chops" who was incarcerated in Leavenworth. I'd felt sorry for her when she'd insisted she just wanted to communicate with him as his "wife," and that the authorities wouldn't let her. Sara Jane didn't want her letter screened by the prison censors who would, I learned later, intercept it because letters between prisoners in different prisons were forbidden. At the time, though, it never dawned on me that there was anything wrong with my sending what I understood to be a love letter to him on Sara Jane's behalf. I mean, she was in for life, and he was far away. It didn't seem much different from when as Catholic high schoolers we had tried to slip love letters past the Jesuit censors. After forwarding the letter, however, I received a threatening letter from the Bureau of Prisons informing me that I had broken rules and might end up joining my client in prison. Being an uninformed lunatic, I shot back a letter expressing my outrage that they were reading attorney–client mail in violation of our hallowed legal privilege. I realized, however, that I was probably unwittingly breaking some rule—a rule of which Sara Jane was no doubt keenly aware.

With my heavy manila envelope under my arm, I went through the gate chatting with guards who were now familiar with my client and me. When I got back to my office, I opened the envelope—and out dropped a prison-made shank, a huge, scary knife whose only purpose could be stabbing another human being.

I was scared now for the first time. Was Sara Jane setting me up? If I had handed it back to her, and it was caught on tape,

I could have been charged with smuggling a weapon into a federal prisoner and faced the loss of my license as well as a felony conviction and imprisonment myself. I would have had a hard time proving I was handing something back to her rather than delivering it to her in the first place. Who was I dealing with, here? Was it just Sara Jane, or were others involved?

I knew from press reports that she had been very involved in People In Need, a food giveaway program for the poor, and that in that role, she had also reportedly acted as a snitch and an informant for both the police and FBI. It seemed that she played both sides of the legal fence. It was all the same to her. Perhaps I had too much time on my hands, or the din of three little kids was impairing me, but I was suspicious of my own client's intentions toward me. For all the months on this case I had been dancing my way through a virtual minefield, and now I was beginning to realize I might be involved in something dangerous—not only to me, but also to my children.

# CHAPTER 5

# LOSING MY BALANCE

By the time I was just over a year into my law career, I was having a love affair with my mentor, a married man eight years my senior.

I met Travis when I went to see his sister, Maureen, for advice. I understood she was an active feminist as well as a lawyer, and when I called her she invited me to come meet with her over lunch. Maureen was one of very few women lawyers with their own practices, and I needed to learn what I could about starting out. I had no idea what I was doing, just that I was going to do something. For good luck, I was decked out in the outfit I had worn to my swearing-in ceremony: a burgundy velvet riding coat over a pink cashmere sweater and matching pink wool slacks. We met in the office suite she shared with her brothers, who were also her law partners. Then, for the first of what turned out to be hundreds of times, she collected her brothers/partners from their offices and we headed over to Coco's, a nearby coffee shop, for lunch.

Maureen, who had no children, sounded as if she spent all her free hours playing competitive tennis, and she looked like it, too. All three, then in their late thirties, were good looking, charming, and charismatic. They enjoyed each other like best friends, lovingly ribbing each other, and even then I sensed that their sibling relationship might be the paramount one in their lives. Their office was like their clubhouse, and Coco's the local drive-in where the "waitstaff" (a gender-neutral term I first heard from Maureen) greeted them warmly. These were definitely the cool kids on campus. They commandeered one of the larger tables to accommodate other local lawyers who knew this was the place to be for up-to-the-minute legal gossip. On this first occasion there were at least ten people. Waiters just kept coming back and filling up whatever coffee cups were on the table, occasionally clucking at the chaos—and, no doubt, at the presumptuousness of the gang of lawyers. The joke was that the bill for the table was actually for rent because we were there so often and so long.

When Travis asked what I wanted to do, I told him I wanted to try cases. He asked if I had applied for any jobs, and I told him I had but was considering all my options. I also told him I had taken the tests for both the district attorney and public defender's offices, and had tested high, but that both offices had hiring freezes because of budget restraints. A small local firm had interviewed me as well, I told him, and they were checking my references before making me an offer. He laughed and said, "You should be checking theirs." Then he invited me back to his office to talk some more.

I had come to talk with Maureen, hoping she might hire me or point me in the right direction, but Travis seemed to be the one in charge. He told me the senior partner at the firm where I had interviewed would drive me crazy with nitpicking, and that the firm was not especially well thought of. Then he offered me space to rent within his firm's offices, insisting I should set up my own practice. To top it off, he made me an offer I couldn't refuse: three months' free rent, a secretary, and my name on the door. A place to be a real lawyer. Flattered, and eager to be in such a vibrant environment, I snapped up Travis's offer and hung out my shingle underneath theirs. I became a solo practitioner.

After that, I consulted Travis on everything I did. In contrast to the men I'd grown up with, he egged me on, told me to go for it, and I liked it. He taught me the ins and outs of practicing law. Here was a man who sought to include rather than exclude me, who thought I had something valuable to say, and who wanted to back me up as I ventured onto the legal battlefield. He vouched for me with the boys' club and took me to bar meetings with him. For the first time, I thought, ignoring our developing love affair, my gender didn't seem to be a handicap.

On the home front, since my poker-playing husband had started coming home later and later, and some nights not at all, I rationalized my office romance. I told myself I was still in love with my husband, even as I fell mindlessly into a relationship that would forever change my life. Denial was key to carrying on like this: denial that my behavior was harming others; denial that I had any control over it; and denial that my paramour had anything other than my best interests at heart.

Then one day I walked out of the courtroom where I had just won the criminal trial defending the flasher, and found Travis talking to my jurors.

"She works in my office," I heard him say.

"I don't work in your office," I told him after the jurors had moved on. "You have no business talking to my jury about my case."

"Geez!" he said, looking wounded. "With you I have to walk on eggshells." A familiar old queasy feeling came over me, and suddenly Travis was much like the men I had grown up around. Yet I didn't stop the affair, and I repressed all my feelings of not only anger but also guilt and shame. I was certainly not the first woman to become romantically involved with her mentor; our romance was probably a cliché, much like the boss taking up with his secretary. In my mind, however, it was entirely different and therefore more acceptable. Looking back, I don't even recognize myself.

When Travis saw the shank Sara Jane had given me, he turned it over in his hands admiringly and suggested I stash it; at some point in the future, he said, when I was no longer on the Moore case, it would be cool to frame it and hang it in my office as a memento. So that became my plan. I also believed what he said about his marriage being on the rocks; whatever he told me was gospel. We continued on and off over several more months in this sordid affair, and I buried my guilt and shame deep within my aching soul. Even when our relationship was no longer happy, and we acknowledged that to each other, we continued on.

Our attraction was impossible to suppress. We had lunch and drinks together nearly daily, hashing over cases and legal gossip with relish. I was under Travis's spell, and when he told me I was brilliant and beautiful, and destined to be a great trial lawyer, I believed him. He made himself totally available to me, made me feel safe and protected as I took on the world. I had found a man in my profession who was on my side. As much as I distrusted the men of my childhood, I trusted him.

So I took my precious prison shank home and hid it from the kids. Perhaps I would've even framed it some day . . . had it not disappeared from my house a few months later.

I was arriving home with the kids when I saw that the sliding glass patio doors were open and the gauzy green tiebacks were loose and billowing into the living room. Instinct prompted me to herd the kids back into the car and down the driveway. We headed for the park and maybe some ice cream. Our Palos Verdes neighborhood had had several follow-home robberies lately, and I was sure that's why I felt jumpy. After an hour or so, we went back home. Everything looked fine. The patio doors were closed and nothing appeared amiss. I must have imagined it, I thought. But a bit later I discovered that Sara Jane's gift to me, the well-hidden prison knife, was gone.

A few weeks later I sat alone at counsel table for Sara Jane, wearing the elegant new beige knit jacket dress and high heels I'd splurged on at an upscale boutique in Palos Verdes. Sara Jane was not there—the federal authorities had deemed her appearance unnecessary. It didn't occur to me to question this decision. I was on unfamiliar turf. Defendants I had represented in state courts had always been brought to the trial court for hearings without my ever requesting it.

Though Sara Jane was not present, across the aisle sat US Attorneys James Browning and Steele Langford, armed with boxes of papers. These men looked right at home, while I sat in awe of even being allowed to make an appearance. As they hadn't filed an opposition, I was surprised that they were allowed to appear and argue at all. But it turned out they didn't have to say anything.

This was my first appearance in federal court anywhere, so I had to go through the formality of having a member of the federal bar in the Northern District appear with me before a judge of that court and make a motion that I be admitted to that bar. I had struggled unsuccessfully to find a local lawyer to do me the professional courtesy of making that pro forma motion—which should have tipped me off that this was not just another case and not just another court. When I could find no one who would do that for me in this case, the judge's secretary told me to just stand up and move my own admission, and that is what I did.

After granting my admission, Judge Conti swiftly denied my ambitious habeas corpus motion, calling our expert psychiatrist, and me, "soldiers of fortune"—an epithet I couldn't help smiling at, although I knew it was meant to be derisive. *At least soldiers of fortune do exciting stuff*, I thought. Judge Conti could have denied the motion without a hearing . . . especially since he had no intention of seriously considering setting aside the judgment and life sentence. But he wanted to appear fair, and granting a hearing accomplished that.

Sara Jane insisted on filing an appeal to the Ninth Circuit Court of Appeal, so I figured out how to do it at what turned out to be the last possible moment. During coffee with my compatriot lawyers one morning, I discovered that the deadline for filing an appeal notice in federal court is ten days, not the thirty days I assumed. Without finishing my coffee, I raced back to my office, grabbed a yellow legal pad, and wrote out the notice in long hand. After my secretary typed it up, I sped to the airport to catch a plane north, and barely made it to the filing window before it closed. I wasn't going to give Sara Jane, a woman who liked a ruckus and notoriety and who had nothing to do for the rest of her life, a claim against me for legal malpractice.

# CHAPTER 6

# "FOR A SMART GIRL,

# YOU SURE DO DUMB THINGS"

It was fall 1977. One cool evening in October, still in high heels and suit from my day in trial, I found myself among the pumpkins in the Halloween Pumpkin Patch with Erin, Colin, and Bronwyn. I was exhausted, with aching legs and a fatigue that made me wonder how I could last through the selection of three perfect pumpkins.

This exhaustion that made me want to lie down right there among the pumpkins began to feel old and familiar, and not necessarily related to my long day. *Oh God! Am I pregnant?*

*My life is in shambles*, I thought as I watched my three children race around the lot, squealing and jumping into haystacks. *I deserve to suffer for what I have done.* I may even have silently said the Act of Contrition at that moment, overcome with guilt and shame as I was. Something had to give. But I could not ruin the joy my little guys had in picking out and carving the pumpkins and then roasting the seeds, a cozy ritual we had that signaled the start of the fall and winter holiday season; I made it through the rest of the evening.

I still had cases and kids to manage. There was no time for self-pity. If I was pregnant I would have to deal with it, making sure I was home more with the three I already had as I prepared for a fourth. And my practice would have to be streamlined to make that happen. So the Sara Jane Moore case could no longer be a priority in my life, especially since the hazards of being involved with her were mounting. Not only did she call my office or home whenever she felt like and demand instant access to me, her antics had started to put me in jeopardy. I recalled the uneasiness I felt when I discovered she used me to smuggle out that prison-made contraband knife. I could no longer justify fighting for this woman—not with another baby on the way.

Sara Jane was decidedly unhappy with my decision. But when she realized I was serious, she wrote to me expressing her understanding and promptly substituted herself in for me. As her own lawyer, Sara Jane set about appealing the ruling denying my motion to set aside the judgment and conviction with the Ninth Circuit Court of Appeal.

*   *   *

Walking back to the office from coffee one morning, Travis told me that his wife was pregnant. I was dumbstruck as I realized that all along he had been lying about the state of his marriage. Using me. The wind knocked out of me, I revealed that I was pregnant, too. Travis took a step closer, looked me in the eye and said, "Are you sure? Have you been to the doctor?" When I answered that I hadn't, he looked relieved. "If you find out you're not, let me know." Then, landing one last blow, he added, "Whose baby is it?"

Mortified for being the fool who'd fallen for the oldest line in the playbook of cheating husbands, I slapped myself back to reality. There was a time when Travis and I had talked about marriage—about leaving our respective spouses and, somehow, being together. But that time was past. We'd dismissed the plan as unrealistic. In fact, we had pretty much ended the affair around the time I conceived.

I answered simply: "Mine."

Travis just stared at me, open-mouthed.

A week earlier, I'd told my husband, Ron, of my pregnancy. His response—"That is not my baby"—told me what I already knew: our marriage was over. I was soon to be a single mother of four.

I felt deep guilt for cheating, especially as I realized that Ron, my once beloved husband, had been moving in another direction for some time. He was gone most evenings, and any money we had seemed to evaporate. When the electricity was turned off one Friday afternoon a week later, I just watched, stunned. The life we'd built was collapsing around us. *What happened to us?* I wondered. *When did my husband become someone who goes alone to casinos? How did I, a married mother of three little kids, become "the other woman"?*

I knew I was acting like a rebellious sixteen-year-old, taking risks and being impulsive. But when I was sixteen I'd been the model of Catholic girl decorum, planning on entering the convent. Now here I was, an unredeemed Mary Magdalene.

At my mother's urging, I asked Ron to move out one night when he slipped in around 5 A.M. His hours were becoming strange enough that Mom and I were both beginning to fear for my safety. When Ron resisted, Mom hung up—she'd stayed on the line just in case—and called my friend Maryann, who lived down the street. Moments later, Maryann walked in the front door with her college Shakespeare textbook under her arm. A few minutes after that, my older brother, Tim, got on the phone with Ron—and finally he left, moving into the little Hermosa Beach house we were remodeling for a resale.

By March 1978—before the baby, Seamus, was born—Ron and I had for the most part struggled through the immediate day-to-day issues of the separation and divorce, including visitation (or what is now more aptly called "shared custodial time"). Our lawyers shepherded us through the technical aspects of amicably ending our marriage as we struggled with the emotional trauma of a family torn apart. We still loved each other, but there was no going back to the way things were.

We tried to still be a family, though. That spring we celebrated Easter with the celestial symphony of the sunrise service at the Hollywood Bowl. It couldn't have been easy for Ron, but legally, because my unborn baby was conceived during our marriage and while we were living together, my husband was irrefutably the baby's father. Our divorce settlement agreement listed the baby as a child of our marriage as legally required, one of four. (That law is different today, and paternity can be challenged under certain circumstances.)

I was awarded our Palos Verdes house, and Ron was awarded two little houses we owned in Hermosa Beach, one of which had become his home, and an apartment building we'd bought in Hawthorn. All that remained was entry of the final judgment. But as one chapter closed, another one that would last a lifetime was just opening. Seamus was born on May 9, 1978. There was no avoiding the facts, especially as the *two* babies, a brother and sister who would never know each other, were born in the same hospital two days apart, and spent a night in bassinets in the same nursery. While I was in labor, a nurse came to tell me, "Mr. Travis is in the waiting room, and he says you want him in with you." I told her I didn't know any Mr. Travis. She came back and said, "He says he is the father." Hurt and emotional, I replied, "No, he isn't."

It was a sentence that would have permanent consequences. But I don't know that I could have done it any other way. Maybe I had created this circumstance to prove I didn't need a man in my life to have a family. Maybe I just wanted to avoid the trap in which I believed my mother and so many other women had been caught. That night in the hospital, one of my mother's favorite catchphrases, always pithy and to the point, echoed in my head: "For a smart girl, you sure do dumb things."

I was about to get even dumber.

## · CHAPTER 7 ·

# STRIKE TWO

Unchastened by a failed first marriage and a disastrous extra-marital affair, I waited only a few months before I married on the rebound. Before my fourth child was a year old, I met a man I will call Jack on a ski trip. My sister Katie, who was staying with me and taking care of the kids, had cajoled me into going on the trip, insisting I needed to get back out in the world. Jack was an attorney too, and we traded courtroom war stories and skied together all weekend.

He was an ambitious and wily litigator employed by a Century City firm; he was also a single father of three teenage boys. He seemed to really love my kids right away, and offered to help organize my office, even bringing in his secretary to set up a filing system. Within a month he suggested marriage. "We should team up and put the whole circus under one tent," he said. It felt good to be taken care of, so I agreed.

Although I was the one who practiced family law, Jack drafted a premarital agreement converting "all the property either of us owns into community property to be owned equally by both of us." In other words, both my house *and* my law practice were now part his, and his house would become our community property. "In the event of the death of either of us," the agreement further provided, "it is the non-binding expectation that each of us will treat the children of the other as children of the marriage." The agreement was the opposite of the typical premarital agreement, and the clause about the children made no sense—not for me or for my children, who had a father. At the time, however, I thought it made sense to pool all our assets and responsibilities, so I agreed.

I sold my Palos Verdes house and put the proceeds into a new joint account Jack had set up, and as soon as school let out in June, just three months after I'd met him, the kids and I moved to his house in Pacific Palisades. The only explanation I have for doing this is that I was numb from the ruin of my first marriage and no longer trusted myself in matters of the heart, or much of anything else. Jack was smart and persuasive. Against my better judgment, I trusted his. I knew I was not in love with him. But I thought my kids, whom he seemed to love, needed a family that at least looked conventional. I told myself I had forfeited the right to love when I cheated on my first husband, and I would learn to love Jack. Could my mother learn to love him, I wondered?

Not unless I got an annulment, she reported. Since my first marriage had taken place before a priest, I could not remarry in the Catholic Church. My parents were in an uproar.

"You're killing your father," my mother told me when I phoned her with the news. "You need to fix this."

At their directive, I telephoned a well-connected priest who instructed me to visit one of the young priests from the marriage tribunal at the Los Angeles Archdiocese. "It is like a court," he told me. "Talk to the priest and ask for his help. He'll go back and tell the tribunal, 'There's a doll out here with a bad marriage.'"

*Did this priest just call me a doll?* A wave of nausea passed over me and I declined. I couldn't subject myself to priests playing lawyer and judge over my life.

Four months after meeting him and one year after my divorce, I married Jack in a glass church in Palos Verdes without a Catholic Church annulment. My fourth child was fourteen months old. Jack's were fifteen, sixteen, and eighteen. My parents refused to come, but I made it as festive as I could, with me and the girls decked out in new dresses, hats, and gloves, and my boys, even the baby, in little tuxedos. All seven kids participated in the ceremony, which was followed by brunch at the Beverly Hills Hotel.

When we went to Ireland for our honeymoon, my parents took care of my kids. As disappointed as they were, I knew they still loved me and their grandchildren.

\*　　\*　　\*

At first, life in our merged families was fun. We went bike riding with my kids along the beach on the weekends and played baseball and basketball at Rustic Canyon Park. The kids did well in their new schools and made lots of new friends. The house was usually packed with the kids and their friends

But about a year and a half into my marriage, I got my first hint that my Brady Bunch fantasy was not quite what it appeared. We started a major construction project on the house, including a brick patio with Jacuzzi, a tennis court, and a pool. Once again, notwithstanding what had happened financially in my first marriage, I abdicated all financial control to my husband. I'm not sure why I was surprised to learn, as we began the renovation process, that Jack had not changed the deed on the house. It was only when the bank required both our names to get a construction loan that he finally put the house in both our names, insisting he had just overlooked it. The deed "oversight" opened my eyes . . . but things continued to get more complicated.

After some contretemps between Jack and Ron over child support payments, Ron stopped paying his court-ordered child support altogether. I was surprised to see Jack become as irate as he did. But then I realized he relied on the $1,200 per month child support as part of our joint income. Jack convinced me to file an enforcement action against Ron for failure to pay pursuant to the court order. Even though the contempt action was legally warranted, I never anticipated that the judge would send him to jail. And once the court held him in contempt and remanded him to custody, there was nothing I could do about it. I had been willfully blind to my own cruelty, compounding my earlier marital betrayal of Ron. As soon as it was done, I would have done anything to undo it. This was not the life I had set out to build. I was not an independent woman; I was someone who did what I was told. Somehow, whenever I found myself in a new relationship, I lost the very thing I had spent my life fighting to protect: my autonomy. As I spent that Christmas filled with regret over what I'd done to Ron, I came to terms with the fact that I didn't have a clue how to be my own woman.

Then Jack's troubled middle son was arrested and prosecuted for residential burglaries he allegedly performed to support his drug habit. He had already stolen and sold my sterling silver and my moped, and had taken my car without permission one night and driven it into a tree, totaling it. His criminal proceedings consumed our household for the better part of a year until, in lieu of a felony conviction and prison, he was sent away to the California Conservation Corps, where he could earn the expungement of his felony conviction.

The legal tumult of our lives took a toll on our relationship and our financial resources. While constant personal involvement in litigation, including with next-door neighbors, seemed to be Jack's natural habitat, I soon realized it was not mine. Our home life was constantly under siege; there was no peace.

In the midst of it all, I learned that Jack was having an affair with one of his secretaries. Living in my own glass house, I could not very well throw stones. But I realized I had to get out. I filed for divorce after only three years of marriage.

Our divorce was brutal, and it consumed another three years of my life, including a ten-day trial. Along with the contention that our prenuptial agreement precluded me from divorcing him, Jack asserted an interest in my law practice and filed liens in my pending cases to intercept any settlements. He also claimed a right to custodial time with my children—and in a bizarre twist, Ron showed up in court to testify on Jack's behalf. His anger at me made sense, but this move did not. At this point, court reporters and other court personnel who knew me approached me in the hallway and said, "What were you thinking?"

I'm not sure I had a thought in my head. Contrary to all the advice I had given my clients, I'd put myself in a serious and unnecessary legal bind with this marriage, undermining the autonomy and independence I had just achieved after leaving Ron. Like the powerless mother I strove not to be, I had abdicated control of my money, signing a premarital agreement that made everything I owned community property. With another lawyer! Before he was even my husband, I'd named Jack the sole beneficiary of a double indemnity life insurance policy and sole beneficiary of my will and trust, "with the non-binding expectation" that he would take care of my minor children should anything happen to me.

Fortunately, I had chosen to not have children with this man, so when the judgment in my favor was affirmed—after several years—I was finally able to move on.

My mother had warned me that marrying Jack was a mistake. Aside from the mortal sin, she could tell I was " going to get hurt." And she was there for me when that day came, three years later. During one of our early-morning phone calls a week after I filed for divorce, my mother urged me to move out that morning, while Jack was out boating for the day, and avoid a confrontation. By early afternoon, with the help of a few friends and a client who worked with longshoremen and had access to trucks, I put my furniture in storage until I could find a new home. Then, exhausted, I went to Palos Verdes to stay with my old friend Maryann—who, along with my mother, had been with me on that other early morning four years before, at the end of my first marriage. Both of these women had seen warning signs I couldn't see. Signs both had pointed out to me. But I had been so vigilant in avoiding danger from one direction that I'd failed to see the traffic coming from the other.

# CHAPTER 8

# THE CHRISTMAS TRIALS

In September 1982, shortly after filing for divorce from Jack, I moved with my four kids to a rental house in Santa Monica Canyon. The new house provided a safe port in the storm of the preceding five years, which had been tumultuous for our whole family. We had survived my affair, a divorce, a new baby, a remarriage, and a second divorce, along with moves to three different homes. Chaos dominated my life as I made one impulsive choice after another, all of them with major life consequences. Desperately, I tried to regain some control and normalcy, which seemed just beyond my reach. Every choice I made seemed to compound our problems.

Holiday traditions provided one constant we could hang on to, so no matter how hard it was, I embraced all of it. Gingerbread day was a big deal at our house. Each kid and their gaggle of friends designed, cut out, and decorated twelve-inch-tall characters in whatever way he or she chose.

One evening, a little more than a week before Christmas, bits of dried gingerbread and sugar crunched under my feet. Tubes of green and red icing, broken candy canes, and saucers with the last morsels of Red Hots, gumdrops, M&Ms, and strings of red licorice lay abandoned on the long trestle table. One-of-a-kind gingerbread characters laden with inch-thick icing and candy faces, glasses, dresses, and scarves lay toe-to-toe along all the counters, a small Christmas army. We had dragged a huge noble fir through the front door a day earlier. The tree sat lighted in the corner of the living room across from the fireplace, wires and nails securing it to the wall (a precaution I'd decided to take after Bridget, our new Samoyed puppy, ran through it and pulled the strings of lights, ornaments, and tree itself down in a tangle). Although I was anxious about an imminent criminal trial in San Diego, I allowed myself to relax, sort of, into the annual festivities.

This annual cookie mess made me happy—surely a measure of the brain damage kids inflict on their mothers. This year's Christmas cookie party for my four (now ages thirteen, ten, nine, and four) and many of their friends was officially over, and the friends had gone home, several with cookie dough in their hair.

I switched off all the downstairs lights except those twinkling on the tree, kicked off my shoes, and sank into the couch in front of the fire with a Waterford tumbler of Jameson's on the rocks. Handel's "Messiah" played on the stereo. Classical music settled my soul and helped me focus.

It was Sunday night, just over a week since the verdict in my last case—a wrongful death suit on behalf of two little girls whose father had been killed in a logging accident in the mountains of Northern California. I was exhausted because I had also played host for that one: my client and her kids had stayed at my house during trial because their home was far away, they were poor, and I couldn't afford to house them anywhere else. To make matters worse, Jack had repeatedly hauled me into court over the past four months, trying to take control of my law practice and its income. It seemed he couldn't resist using every legal weapon in his arsenal—which, I suppose, I should have expected after hearing him describe his strategy for winning any case: "Attack, attack, attack!"

During one post-trial hearing, my opposing counsel informed me that Jack had phoned and demanded his name be included in any recovery, a legal absurdity since he was not counsel in the case. Opposing counsel insisted he and I have a chambers conference with our judge because my ex had also warned him he planned to show up in court that morning.

The clerk led us into chambers. Judge Bigelow stood in front of his bookcase, a book in hand. When we explained what was going on, Judge Bigelow smiled slightly and said, "I hope I won't have to put Jack in jail." I was happily surprised: this judge was going to protect me. My embarrassment over my ex-husband's meddling vanished. For the rest of the trial, I forgot about Jack and embraced the intellectual discussions about case law and other legal authority that came up between me and the opposing counsel. This trial was a peak moment in my career: it was the moment I realized that adversaries—even male adversaries—could be honorable. When settlement was finalized, he even offered to meet in a grocery store parking lot to exchange the money before my ex could do anything further to interfere. I left that trial with renewed faith: in the legal system, in myself, and in men.

Yet my home life had become just the opposite. I was now truly alone. In supporting my kids. In navigating their worlds. An evening of rocking a child and singing my full repertoire of Irish lullabies preceded early-morning trips to the jail to see clients before court. Or a sleepless night of soothing sick kids turned into a morning charging through the courthouse doors or into a deposition and blasting my opponent with both barrels—sometimes, it seemed, just to stay awake through the proceedings. Sleeping during this time was nearly impossible. I spent most nights praying the rosary—allowing my grandmother's beautiful silver beads to soothe me.

But this Christmas, as this rare moment of solitude dissolved along with the ice in my Waterford tumbler, I remembered I had to leave before dawn for my next trial in San Diego. I jumped up; I hadn't gotten to the cleaners! Was there any chance the jury wouldn't be offended by five days of the same suit? The best I could do was pray I would be the beneficiary of the much-hyped generosity of Christmastime jurors. Even so, I'd have to find an all-night convenience store for a supply of panty hose on my way south. Those things shredded like confetti.

For the first few days of trial, especially during jury selection and in front of a conservative judge, I always wore demure skirt suits or dresses and pumps, as well as my expired wedding ring, to present as little distraction as possible in courts not yet fully adjusted to women warriors. Only after I established identification with my jurors, the judge, and other courtroom personnel would I put my guard down enough to reveal myself by, say, wearing pantsuits and jewelry. But I had only one clean skirt suit this time around, so that would be my uniform for the week.

Before heading upstairs and falling into bed that night (or, more accurately, that morning), I pulled out my "prime exhibit" for the next morning's trial: a layout of the hotel, really more of a transient flophouse, where the shooting had taken place. I would have to persuade the jury that my client, Susan, whose paranoia was obvious to any passerby, had thought she was being attacked and acted in self-defense when she shot a young woman with a midnight special .22-caliber handgun.

Susan's gun had been concealed in her bag, along with a spinach soufflé recipe torn from the newspaper. The recipe now had a hole shot through the middle of it. So did her bag. An identical but non-deadly wound had been suffered by the alleged victim, one of the street kids who'd taunted her.

Susan was a colorful young bag lady whose wealthy Milwaukee family had hired me to defend her. When the prosecutor asked her to identify her bag and its contents, Susan reached into the bag, pulled out the tattered bit of newspaper, and read the recipe aloud.

The jury was charmed: they gave us an acquittal after only one hour of deliberations. Susan, who exuded a gamey street smell, threw her arms around me right there in the courtroom and gave me a bear hug, her thick old brown knee-length cardigan adding to the bear effect. I felt an odd combination of jubilation and loneliness as I accepted her hug. I loved the win; and as a woman in a male-dominated profession, I could somehow identify with lonely women like Susan, the "official" outsiders. As I walked her to the bus to say good-bye, I wondered how often she got to hug another person or be hugged by one. But she smiled at me and yelled, "Merry Christmas!" as she climbed onto the bus.

When her bus pulled away, I made a beeline back to the Holiday Inn, packed up my bags, and headed up the San Diego Freeway. It was a classic hot, sunny, and windswept Santa Ana December day. Clear blue skies and pounding surf created big rainbow sprays in the wind along the shore. Winning was sweet—especially today, as I raced home for Christmas.

It was December 23, and I had not yet shopped for the kids. I swung by Pep Boys on the way home and wrote a check for four shiny new bikes. They would consume all the empty space under the tree. I knew I risked bouncing that check, but I also knew I would somehow come up with the money to cover it.

I arrived home to an empty house, and sat down to savor a rare quiet moment. It didn't last. Gloria, my secretary, called within the hour with a potential new client—a Pakistani importer who was staying at a hotel near my office in Torrance. A car had run down his messenger, who transported valuable jewels from Pakistan to sell in the United States. Accidentally, according to the customs broker . . . three times . . . near the customs broker's office. Now the jewels, as well as Oriental rugs and electronics my potential client was importing, were all missing, and he wanted to go after the broker.

When I met with the client, he handed me $5,000 in cash. Exhausted though I was, I was in no position to turn him down. I made plans to file his case within a few days, and told him I had to leave for another appointment. Then I took the $5,000 cash retainer straight to the bank to cover the check I had written for the bikes.

*   *   *

In 1986 I had back-to-back trials right up till Christmas, both involving shootings in venues we mothers typically associate with kids and fun: one at a McDonald's, and the other just outside Magic Mountain. My McDonald's client, Sylvia, was working after school when two armed robbers stormed in and ordered everyone to lie facedown on the floor. Sylvia moved and was shot in the side. She suffered serious ongoing stomach problems, and there was a question whether she would ever be able to bear children. I learned during our investigation that to robbers, fast food at McDonald's means fast cash. Everyone knew the stores were run by kids, were cash only, and were laid out ideally for a fast getaway. I was shocked when I discovered that corporate headquarters actually kept statistics on crimes in their restaurants, which I took as proof that the probability was at least one robbery per year in every restaurant.

I built my case on what I alleged was a dangerous design by the fast food empire. Failing to warn Sylvia that there had already been two robberies in the months before she was hired was negligence. My motherly instincts were roused. It seemed reasonable to expect that a company that made millions on the backs of kids like Sylvia should be forced to take reasonable action, including installing security cameras—and when those failed, and they got shot at work, that they should compensate them appropriately. I advised Sylvia to reject a settlement offer of $75,000.

The jury seemed troubled by the known frequency of robberies at McDonald's, graphically shown on blowups of reported incidents kept by McDonald's home office in Illinois. And our forensic safety expert was great—there was almost no cross-examination from the defense. Perhaps most importantly, they liked Sylvia.

Each day I watched as our trial judge went to lunch with Judge Bigelow from the next courtroom over, the judge before whom I had tried the logging death case a few years before. Judge Bigelow was, to me, the paragon of judicial temperament; conservative, but fair and thoughtful, always fully briefed on the issues and facts and willing to consider all interpretations of the applicable law.

After the presentation of our case, the McDonald's lawyer made a motion for a nonsuit, contending the law required that the case be thrown out no matter what the evidence showed. This motion is standard and, in those days, was usually denied out of hand if there was any substantial evidence to support the plaintiff's case so I wasn't worried—until the judge ordered a lunch recess and said he'd take it "under submission" and rule in the afternoon. Something felt weird and wrong. There was no way would he throw this case out now. Was there?

But then I saw a Judge Bigelow, eyes downturned, return from lunch alone. I got a chill. It didn't take long to find out why: back in the courtroom, the judge granted the motion for nonsuit, ruling that as an employee of the franchise, Sylvia was limited to Workers Compensation. In other words, the big corporation shielded itself with its franchise arrangement (which made her an employee of a third party, the franchisee); yet it brandished the sword of Worker's Compensation statutes as if it were her employer to avoid liability for injuries suffered by her on the job that were, according to their own statistics, predictable.

After extensive research, Judge Bigelow had ruled the opposite way a few years before in the case I'd tried before him. In that case, the logger was killed while working for a subcontractor, and Judge Bigelow found that a known risk inherent in a specific work environment created what was known as a non-delegable duty. Different courtroom and different judge equals two very different results.

Interestingly, the defense lawyer was not ready to put on any witnesses. Perhaps he knew he wouldn't have to. The sense of unfairness was crushing. In a reverse Superman routine, I raced for the old oak phone booth down the hall, closed the hinged double doors, and promptly fell apart, tears pouring onto the front of my silk blouse. My poor client! I would have to call her at home and explain what made no sense to me. It was a good half hour before I could compose myself enough to leave my hideout without being seen crying by the jurors—who, I could see through the beveled-glass panels, were unhappy at having their days of jury service tossed aside by the judge.

My McDonald's case was more than twenty years ago, a time when the term "tort reform" was just coming into usage. "Tort reform" is misleading shorthand for a campaign undertaken in the mid-eighties by insurance, tobacco, gun, energy, and pharmaceutical companies to eliminate lawsuits against big business by duping the public into believing the myth that "multimillion-dollar verdicts," "runaway juries," "greedy trial lawyers," and an explosion of "frivolous lawsuits" had "broken the civil justice system." As I saw it, the carefully orchestrated campaign quietly enlisted the media to pound away on these demonstrably false accusations to turn the public against lawyers, juries, and, ultimately, their own best interests. Ridiculing injured plaintiffs was key. Remember the McDonald's "burn" case and the ridicule heaped upon the elderly woman who had been burned so severely she required numerous skin grafts? All along she asked only to have her medical expenses covered, and yet she was made out to be a crazy, greedy plaintiff.

This movement in its early stages ambushed us. I had no way of knowing they saw my case as an important one, even though it was against one of the world's largest and most powerful corporations.

*   *   *

At this point in my career, the mid-eighties, I started getting cases that involved gun violence. Suddenly, it seemed, guns were everywhere, and in some of the most unlikely places. Gun violence was becoming part of everyday life. For some people, especially the poorest, this made just going to work or taking a family outing increasingly risky. When the McDonald's trial came to a halt, another one rose into view. Another shooting incident: this time at a popular Chevron.

For no reason we could see, the owner of the gas station just outside Magic Mountain in Southern California had pulled a gun and shot a Hispanic man on his way to the amusement park with his family. And it didn't end there: station employees beat up other members of the man's large Mexican-American family as well.

Like a kid sent to his room to do his homework, I sat in front of my fireplace and sifted through a jumbled box of documents produced by the defendants in discovery. Suddenly, I hit a gold mine: letters of complaints from minority customers spanning several years and creating a documented history of similar attacks by employees who kept chains, bats, and guns on hand to use on random minority customers.

I worked the case for more than a year, jousting my way through long days of depositions with three different firms who represented varying interests in the case. Among them was Tom Dowling, a charming Irishman who was representing the shooter, the station owner. Tom was famous for wooing juries and was the father of my son Seamus's friend; he lived around the corner from us in Santa Monica Canyon. I liked and respected Tom, and was determined that Seamus and John Christopher's friendship would not be impacted by the case.

Seamus loved the idea that I was sparring with his friend's father in court. "Are you gonna beat John Christopher's dad?" he asked every morning as I got him ready for school. "I want you to." Still, I was relieved when Chevron replaced Tom with another lawyer from a big firm—a lawyer who caused the rest of the defense team to gasp audibly when he put his arm around my waist as we walked down the hallway his first day on the case. Now this was a man I wanted to beat up.

As trial approached, I realized that the defense team, some of whom had been in the courtroom along with the tort reformers as I tried the McDonald's case, were counting on my being broke and needing to settle. Their lawyers made an absurdly low offer for all of the plaintiffs combined—one I could not ethically take, even though I was starting to feel some serious financial heat. As a trial lawyer, I was working this case on contingency, meaning I would receive no pay unless and until I settled it or won it and survived an appeal and the years that would take. Worse, I was the sole lawyer in my office in those days, and as such I made no money at all during the days and weeks I was in court. It didn't take a genius, or even an investigator, to see that I was under financial stress, though it's possible that they had done some sleuthing on me; that was becoming uncomfortably common.

In any case, I was at a serious disadvantage going up against Chevron, a major American oil company with unlimited funds for the fight. But I was still idealistic enough to like taking on the big guys on behalf of the little ones.

Chevron offered $250,000 for the whole case—all ten clients—calculating that I couldn't turn it down, but clearly knowing it was not reasonable for the injuries the family had sustained. My cut would've been $80,000, since I had the case on a 30 percent contingency. Eighty thousand would pay a lot of bills and make life easier. It would free me from the long trial and the costs of putting it on. But I couldn't allow myself to sell out my clients. Also, the global offer put me in the spot of having to get all ten clients to agree on how the money should be divided, a move certain to create a conflict of interest among them, and between them and me. I needed to settle, but I couldn't settle for this. We were going to trial. Or rather, my clients were—I no longer had the resources to fight. I turned the trial over to another attorney and his firm. It felt a bit like asking a big brother to step in, but I had to do it.

When this powerhouse plaintiff's lawyer, Larry, came aboard, however, he wouldn't hear of my bowing out. We settled the case for a substantial sum (which, by the terms of the set-tlement agreement, I am barred from stating). On that overcast December afternoon, as we walked to the parking lot outside the Van Nuys courthouse, Larry, father of five kids himself, refused to take a fee on the case. "Now your kids can have a good Christmas," he said. I cried all the way home. Once again, my faith in the system, and in other people, was restored.

When I arrived home, seven-year-old Seamus, who had been in bed with a sore throat and chest cold for a week, tossed me a new case, flushed and croaking: "I want to sue the doctor for malpractice," he said. "He didn't make me better . . . I'm still sick."

"Honey, just because you didn't get better right away doesn't mean the doctor committed malpractice," I responded gently.

"You discriminate against kids!" Seamus shot back. He was in no mood for my civics lecture about the role of courts and the necessity of a case actually having merit. I lay down on my bed, which he had commandeered, and I shared with him the events of the day and how ugly real discrimination is. He thought about it and agreed to reconsider his case against both his doctor and me.

\*     \*     \*

My kids and I found camaraderie and laughter in some very unlikely places in those days. In the Christmas season of 1989, I was in trial on an AIDS discrimination case. My client, Elise, had grown up in extreme poverty in a New York ghetto, joined the Army, and then found out through blood tests that she had HIV. She came to me because she was being harassed by her boss at a security company at Los Angeles International Airport (LAX). Was the harassment about her illness? It was unclear but likely, based on other AIDS cases I had handled. When he found out she had AIDS, he tried to make her life so difficult she would quit.

AIDS was at the time a recognized disability under the law, meaning Elise was entitled to reasonable accommodation for her illness, including time away from work for medical appointments. Although she was still able to perform the essential functions of her job and was not yet symptomatic, her company was actively trying to interfere with her medical appointments. I filed what was known as "constructive termination" for Elise, used when an employer was making an employee's life so difficult that a reasonable person under similar circumstances would feel compelled to resign. (Elise made a brilliant observation when she said, "Ms. G., there's nothing constructive about it! It's *de*structive, if you ask me.")

During jury selection, Colin brought Seamus to court to watch. They arrived with a plate of homemade chocolate chip cookies while we were doing *voir dire*: picking a jury. This is a crucial part of trial, because the lawyers get to engage the potential jurors directly, and there are always surprises. I pointed out to the panel, as I always do, that they were giving me noncommittal answers the same way my kids often did, and that I understood their not wanting to be singled out for questioning. I also told them I was used to getting "uh-huh" and "uh-uh," but would prefer a bit more.

Among the potential jurors sat a middle-aged cowboy—Western shirt, boots, big silver belt buckle, and cowboy hat in lap—who gave long answers to all questions, purported to hate corporations, and said his hobby was "dating." Everyone listened raptly to his shaggy-dog responses. He was a performer who was clearly going to be a commanding presence during deliberations if he was on the jury. That presented a huge risk for both sides, because it was impossible to tell which way he would swing.

Opposing counsel and I went back and forth in our Ping-Pong match of excusing jurors on peremptory challenges. Neither one of us wanted to risk alienating the rest of the panel by bouncing the cowboy, a distinct risk in the event some of them had connected with him during their down time. But finally, I had to use my last challenge to let him go; he was just too unpredictable. As I stood and said, "The plaintiff thanks and excuses juror number nine," from the back of the courtroom came an audible, "Awwww, Mom . . ."

Seamus and Colin were escorted from the room by the bailiff as the jurors in the box smiled. To this day, Seamus insists that I asked the bailiff to remove them. I suppose it would be handy for all mothers to have a bailiff at the ready.

\*　\*　\*

We rode the roller coaster of Christmas trials through the years the kids were at home and beyond. In 1991, Colin's first year at NYU, I raced to LAX to meet his flight home for Christmas vacation. I had a rented Santa suit in the back of the car, and lots of toys and dolls piled up next to it. I was sure Colin would embrace the spirit of the season and happily dive into my scheme to bring Christmas to some very unfortunate kids.

The airport was filled with college kids and family and Christmas cheer—a jarring contrast to the preceding day, which I had spent at the home of a family of seven kids whose thirty-five-year-old diabetic mother had, along with her baby, died in childbirth the week before. Our medical expert had reviewed the records and opined that there was no medical malpractice case, because the hemorrhaging that took her life was not the delivering doctor's fault. The father had no heart for Christmas, and I'd decided it was my family's turn to give someone else's kids a Christmas. I hoped Colin would see it the same way. He was about to become Santa.

It was a Santa Ana winds–hot day, and after "pulling several all-nighters" cramming for exams, Colin had lost so much weight at school that he was more elf than Santa.

"You're kidding, Mom," he groaned when I told him my plan. He was horrified at the prospect of putting on the Santa suit. Of course, he did need a ride home—and when he recalled how lucky he and his siblings had always been at Christmas, and realized how dreadful the loss of a mother at that time had to be, he got with the plan pretty quickly.

Colin donned the Santa suit and glued on the white beard and eyebrows in the car. To pull off the surprise to maximum effect, I let him out a block from the house. He swung the toy-laden brown velvet sack over his shoulder, simultaneously using both hands to hold his pants up, the way he had in kindergarten, and headed down the street in the hot sun. By the time he arrived at the house, he was not only dripping with sweat and losing his eyebrows and beard, he also had a Pied Piper–size following of small people who were dumbstruck to see Santa actually delivering piles of toys.

Once Santa had doled out the toys, I joined the gathering. Soon, the sad house full of grieving adult relatives came alive with the sound of happy kids playing in the yard with their new toys. With a last "ho ho ho," Santa walked back down the block and I followed. Now Santa could go home and relax after his finals!

\*   \*   \*

I could stuff a flock of turkeys with all the papers I was served during the holidays by the big firms who kept round-the-clock word processors plowing ahead at full-tilt. On the evening before Thanksgiving in 1993, as I was making pies and preparing the turkey in a house full of kids on school break, two burly process servers/investigators showed up at my front door. The French door–style kitchen window was at a right angle to the entry, putting them in full view of the whole room and I immediately recognized them from their many trips to my office.

*Oh,* I realized, *it's the "We know where you live" tactic.*

As my kids and their friends looked on, the goon squad served me with a defamation lawsuit, naming me personally as the defendant. IBM was suing me for answering questions posed by a *Wall Street Journal* reporter and other media who were covering the case I was working. They were also furious that my client, Veronica, had told a network television reporter that she was "hooking for IBM." She said it with me sitting right there next to her. I almost fell off my chair on that one, too, but the truth wasn't all that far off.

Around the same time, after Veronica ripped off her microphone and stormed out of a deposition when IBM's lawyer asked her if she had ever had an abortion, IBM messengered me a letter saying that her behavior led them to believe that both the attorneys and IBM might be in danger from her. Next they demanded that the deposition immediately resume, and that one of their New York lawyers be allowed to attend the next session of my client's deposition by phone, citing his wife's imminent due date and his doubling as labor coach and snow shoveler should the New York snowstorms continue. I couldn't restrain my inner smart-ass in my response. I pointed out that I had given birth myself four times with less fanfare, and wrote back, "Even Joseph had a better plan for Mary 2,000 years ago, and I too need a shovel after reading your letter."

IBM's lawyers were furious and made a motion for sanctions against me, citing my client's walking out of the deposition and my lack of cooperation in resuming it on their terms. Much was made of my snide dismissal of the expectant father. IBM was playing hardball. I was sanctioned $4,900 by the judge—just short of the $5,000 that would have required me to report to the bar—for the incident.

My street-fighter approach to litigation occasionally cost me real money, but it was virtually impossible for me, a sole practitioner, to fight these behemoths on their terms. So I engaged my own guerilla tactics when it seemed necessary. For example, when they and other big law firms bombarded me with unending faxes, my defense was simply to unplug my fax machine.

The IBM trial was brutal, and much was at stake for both sides.

"We want that $50 million contract, and you can get it for us. He helped you get this job." So began the instruction Veronica testified was given her by her female boss at IBM. The "he" was Gary Denman, who had been Veronica's boss when she worked on artificial intelligence as a civilian employee for the Air Force. Denman was now head of the Pentagon's Defense Advance Research Project Agency (DARPA), which was doling out federal millions on technology, the "dividend" at the end of the Cold War. He had also been Veronica's lover as well as her boss while both were employed at the Air Force base in Ohio a few years earlier, and was, according to Veronica's testimony, still in hot pursuit. He had actually helped place her at IBM when he left the base for Washington.

In coming to my home rather than my office the night before Thanksgiving, what the goons were really trying to deliver was intimidation and embarrassment sufficient to make me drop the case. They had not been paying attention, I guess.

I accepted the service papers and went back to my annual cooking frenzy. "Nice try," I said to opposing counsel when she later asked, "So how was *your* Thanksgiving?"

It got so that I couldn't quite imagine a holiday season without litigation involved, so it just added to the excitement.

Admittedly, I had to hide my exhaustion as best I could, and get help where I could find it, too. One year I even hired a caterer for Christmas Eve. Initially I was horrified by my uncharacteristic capitulation, but I wanted the cheery custom, fantasized or not, of a perfectly laid table and traditional dishes, even if I couldn't personally deliver it. And when the caterer met me at the door with an icy martini and led me to a chair in front of the fire, I got over my feelings of feminine failure rather swiftly—by the second martini, anyway. In my memory it was a beautiful, perfect, relaxed Christmas Eve with warm candlelight and family and, as always, random friends around the table.

It wasn't always so easy. Getting to a place where I could snuff out my feelings of failure as a mother and a woman had taken several decades of having to find a way to combine my trial practice with motherhood and having a relationship with a man. About ten years earlier, after two divorces within four years, my life had been in crisis on all fronts as I desperately thrashed around trying to do it all.

## • CHAPTER 9 •

# IT WILL BE ALL RIGHT
# WHEN YOU GET HOME

In May 1984, I went to New York for a long weekend of theater, museums, and fabulous restaurants with Hank, a man I had started seeing about a year earlier. Twenty years my senior, he epitomized the Jewish toast "L'chaim," (to life), seasoning the banalities of life with art, theater, travel, and his version of "fine dining," from the local Nate'n Al deli to the elegant Château la Chèvre d'Or, perched on a mountaintop in the French village of Eze.

Hank moved gracefully through the world without causing ripples, and the world returned the favor. My world, however, was a tidal wave, and I was not moving gracefully through it. My second divorce was still bouncing around in the court of appeals and draining my minimal resources. During the years I was with Hank, by comparison, things always seemed to unfold his way. He never freaked out over cases or let them interfere with his personal life—not even his lunch, and nothing interfered with his sleep. Parking places opened up in impossible places just when he wanted one. While driving through the moonscape-like Irish Burren once, he said, "I'm hungry," and around the next bend we came upon a French restaurant with sculpted butter pats topped with shamrocks. On another trip he sought and found an Irish restaurant in the middle of Paris.

As usual, Hank had thoughtfully arranged every little detail for our trip to New York, including our lovely room at the Carlyle—where, consumed by anxiety, I had lain awake all night. Just before nodding off to sleep, he joked that he could hear the wheels turning in my head. It was no joke. I was stretched to the limit in every aspect of my chaotic life. In the five short years between 1979 and 1984, I had gone through two divorces and moved the kids three times, requiring them to change schools three times as well. Although I played tough and most people couldn't see it, including Hank, I was just barely afloat; the lifeboat full of needy kids that I was paddling was taking on water, and on the verge of capsizing.

Three of my four kids were in their early teens now. At fourteen, the eldest, Erin, was finding me increasingly less cool to be around. She was justifiably not pleased about having to move three times and change schools, either. I was in over my head.

My own teen years in a small midwestern town had been steady, sheltered, and uneventful. I'd planned to enter the convent after high school—and besides, I'd lived in fear of—and dying to please—my mother, so I didn't rock that boat at all. It would have been inconceivable to show anger at my mother or disobey her in any way. In this very different world in which I was raising my kids, I could only speculate on what Erin and her Palisades friends were up to, although they did frequently stay over at our house, giggling late into the night and expecting pancakes in the morning. My sister Katie, ten years younger than I, had recently warned me that Erin's friends were involved in drugs and would pull Erin in or use her in some way. Although this scared me a bit, I saw no evidence that it was true, and I had written it off to Katie's resentment of what she viewed as spoiled rich kids. Even so, I had left her in charge of the kids for the weekend.

And here I was in New York, because I was determined to learn how to be in a relationship with a man, this elegant and thoughtful man who clearly loved my kids and me. What the hell was I doing? I had nothing left in me to give to a new relationship. I wanted to run. Again. I was suffocating, even amidst these luxurious surroundings.

My economic burden was amplified by my decision during my second divorce to stop enforcing the child support order against Ron. I had decided I would find a way to support my children by myself, because I still carried incredible guilt from my betrayals of Ron, and I'd decided my time was better spent on my clients' cases. This is not a policy I promote for other single parents; it's just what made the most sense for me under the circumstances. Perhaps I also still needed to prove that I could do everything on my own. That proof was becoming increasingly hard to come by.

The owners of the Santa Monica home I'd rented since leaving Jack two years earlier were now pressuring me to either buy the home for $600,000—impossible for me—or move out at the end of the lease term in August. Although I did need to buy a house soon to avoid a huge tax bill on my half of the sale proceeds of Jack's and my house (which had been ordered sold), the money was tied up because Jack was appealing the divorce judgment in our case. I found myself unable to leave such worries behind, so they came right along to New York with me and weighed me down.

I had noticed that men didn't seem to struggle with this life balance like I did. Hank had done the single parenting thing too; he had raised four kids on his own after his wife died when his youngest daughter was just ten years old. So I naturally looked to him for occasional wisdom, sometimes as if he were my parent. He was gracious, kind, and thoughtful, and engaged my kids in a genuine way, taking Seamus to get starter jackets for his favorite teams, and popping over to Aahs! with Bronwyn to fetch "Hello Kitty" trinkets. Most of all he was patient and stable, a counter to the wild ups and downs that littered my personal landscape, including impulsive marriages and divorces, financial reckless-ness, and general chaos.

The one thing I'd always been pretty sure of up to this point was my mothering. I felt I knew what I was doing in that depart-ment for the most part, and was good at finding ways to engage with the kids over their daily activities. We left Post-it notes for each other all over the place, and I anticipated and answered requests for permission to do various things. My kids have kept many of those notes, and I marvel now at the energy going back and forth through our scribbles.

On this first morning in New York, however, the dam burst. I was drowning. Inside my head I heard the voice of my mother condemning me as she had whenever I put my wants ahead of hers. "You selfish girl. You think only of yourself." I had been a bad Catholic, an unfaithful wife, and was an imposter as a woman, and now I feared I was becoming a bad mother. Something went off in me; I started sobbing and crumbled to the floor—like Humpty Dumpty, or like the eggshell skull plain-tiff in the law of torts.

The "eggshell skull" doctrine holds that whoever causes the final damage or injury to a person who has been previously injured due to the fault of others, rendering him especially vulnerable, no matter how slight the final blow might be, is responsible for all the injuries the person has suffered, even those they had nothing to do with.

Well, I played all those parts in this play. I was the eggshell skull that crumbled and I was the cause of the crumble, and all that went before it. I had recklessly driven myself to the edge, and now I was going over. I had no business being in New York just to have fun. I had left my kids, ages fourteen, twelve, eleven, and six, to be somewhere I didn't have to or want to be. I became hysterical, and Hank arranged for a one-way ticket home. He would be left with my return flight ticket, as well as theater tickets that he had made a real effort to get. He wasn't happy, but, as always, he accommodated me.

On reflection I realize I was having a spiritual crisis, having internalized all the judgment and shame that Catholicism reserves for wayward girls. I, once the little girl determined to serve the world as a missionary nun who for years had gone to daily Mass and Communion and observed all the rules and rituals of the Church, now found myself with no inner life to sustain me. On the contrary, the teachings and tenets of my Catholic faith condemned me in no uncertain terms, like an unredeemed Mary Magdalene. There are no sins more egregious in Catholicism than the sexual sins of women, and even today, in 2016, the Cardinals and bishops of the Church are fighting Pope Francis, who has proposed softening this opprobrium. Catholics such as I are still banned from full participation in the Church; specifically, we are banned from receiving Communion, if we have divorced and remarried or exercised control over our own reproductive lives by using contraception.

I had regularly and subversively broken those rules, committing yet more mortal sins. I still prayed all the time—but I directed my prayers to the Blessed Mother, as I experienced a connection to a feminine Divine. That belief was also anathema to the Catholic Church, pushing me farther outside the fold.

The taxi ride to the airport was misery. Once strapped into my seat on the plane, I sobbed throughout the trip home. Was I having a nervous breakdown? I tried to numb my pain with whiskey, but that didn't work, so I pulled out my rosary and started to pray, drink, and cry at the same time. And then, as if she were an apparition, a gentle, grandmotherly woman came and sat beside me. Perhaps she was an angel. She took my hand and started to pray with me. I felt a sad, resigned calm come over me when she softly said, "It will be all right when you get home." And then she was gone.

As soon as I walked in the door of my house, I told my sister Katie, who had once again been staying with the kids, that she could go home, that I needed to be alone with my kids. "Well, you won't be alone with them," she said, laughing. "There are a bunch of kids upstairs."

Erin had had her friend Delphine stay over, and they had bleached Erin's hair and cut it so that, with a shake of her head, she could disappear behind it. When Katie pointed it out and asked what I thought of it, I just said, "So what? It's her own hair," adding lightly, "As long as she doesn't do it to mine." The other kids all had friends over too, and, yes, the house was messy and chaotic. But it felt good to me.

I was ill equipped as a floundering single parent of a teenage girl living in the fast lane of Santa Monica. Everything was a secret. She forged my signature to play hooky from school so often that when I actually signed one, they thought it was a forgery. I was screwing this up, and I had three more kids to usher through adolescence. When I got back from New York Erin wouldn't talk to me, and she looked annoyed that I had come home early.

When I shared my maternal insecurities with Hank, he reassured me that Erin and I would be close again, that it was just teen girl stuff. But since my life was all about winning and losing, this felt like I was losing. Worse, I was actually incompetent. I forced Erin to get tested for drugs, which made her more enraged at me. As it should have. I was dead wrong. She was clean. Not even a sign of marijuana in her system. She insisted it was a punishment, telling her siblings, "Don't complain around here or Mom will put you in the Care Unit."

One Saturday morning about ten months later, as I sat at the kitchen table reading the paper, Erin picked up a section that had a full-page ad for a specially priced Mediterranean cruise that included big pictures of the Egyptian pyramids and the Sphinx. More of an artist than a newspaper reader, Erin studied the pictures for a long time. Then she said, "I wish I could go there someday."

"Me too," I replied with a casual smile, thinking, *Oh my god! She's actually talking to me!* I didn't dare be too enthusiastic.

The following Monday, I mentioned that conversation to my secretary, Gloria, who had already navigated the storm of adolescence with a teen girl. The next thing I knew she had brochures from the travel agency that was doing the promotion, and insisted I should just go ahead and buy tickets for all four kids and me, to "celebrate" the end of the divorce. I had finally received my share of the money from the sale of the Pacific Palisades house and had just closed escrow on a three-bedroom house in Santa Monica, with a little money left over. Gloria, a classy British transplant who always dressed in high heels for the office, was happily married and a working mom raising three kids, two of them then in their teens. I trusted her advice. Next thing I knew, I was putting tickets for the cruise on a credit card.

*   *   *

That summer we took the Love Boat (Princess Cruise Lines) tour from Naples through the Greek Islands to Israel and Egypt, and then back to Italy for a stay in Florence and Rome before flying back home. Guided excursions inland were provided at each port of call, and Erin got to see and sketch the pyramids and the Sphinx, the Nile, the Galilee, Jerusalem, and many other mythical and mystical places. Colin and Bronwyn got to stand beside the iconic fountain in Pompeii, the picture of which was on the cover of their Latin book. And Seamus got to run wild on the ship.

The trip was not without its scary moments, in the form of constant catcalls in Italy and aggressive and leering Bedouins in the desert offering to buy my daughters for 300 camels. Erin started hiding under a hooded sweatshirt and bulky clothes after that happened, and huddled close to me on all excursions. At that moment, I knew at some deep level that she once again trusted me.

When Erin asked me to join her at yoga one day, I was moved almost to tears by her invitation. In a studio a few blocks from my office, she had begun studying with an old Santa Monica yogi. I was honored to be invited into her new world. I remember the first afternoon I went—barely breathing as we lay on our backs in *savasana*, eyes closed, my upturned fingertips nearly touching hers, so grateful she had finally reached out to me. My daughter had been developing a genuine spiritual life that I wanted too. This moment would transform my life, as the study and practice of yoga would become part of my very identity.

Erin became a vegetarian, and she occasionally invited me to lunch at Govinda's, a restaurant in West Los Angeles across the street from the Hari Krishna Temple. She now cringingly refers to this time as her "hippie" stage—a time when she was into Grateful Dead concerts and sometimes dragged me off to the Hare Krishna Temple, where we sat on the floor and ate mushy food splashed on paper plates by barefooted devotees. My daughter was bringing me into a world about which I knew nothing, but into which I gladly followed her. I would have followed her anywhere she would let me.

I also followed her lots of places she wouldn't let me, including unchaperoned parties in the Palisades. While I wanted her to experience the fun of high school and knew that was important to her growth and development, I was also fearful of what was to me an unknown and dangerous teen world. My stepsons had gotten involved in drugs in a big way in that world several years earlier. So, with the best of intentions, I made myself a nuisance. It became a standard for the kids to warn each other, "Don't invite Erin, or her mom will come, too."

After I'd been conducting myself like this for months, seeing how pulled apart I felt with the kids moving into their teen years, Hank proposed a plan to move my offices closer to home, from Torrance to Santa Monica: he suggested that we become partners in ownership of a small turn-of-the-century craftsman house on 11th Street in Santa Monica, hire restoration design experts, and relocate both our offices there, so I could be closer to home. This meant dislodging his practice from Beverly Hills, where it had been for thirty-plus years. But we set about restoring the house, and ultimately won a preservation award from the Los Angeles Conservancy for our efforts.

The happiest and most important years of my law practice were spent in that little blue Victorian with the old side-by-side burgundy red doors in the front, one leading up the Persian-carpeted stairs to my office, the other opening into Hank's with the cozy fireplace. I loved bounding up the stairs with a basket of roses

I'd clipped from the rose garden, and how Hank and I popped into each other's office for quick chats throughout the day.

Finally, I seemed to have the setup to merge my work life into my family life and have a healthy relationship with a man, with an office that was not only close to home but also felt like home. Kids and dogs would drop by unannounced, and, likewise, I would pop home just as unannounced. By the end of Erin's high school years, I felt as if I pretty much had the balanced life I had been seeking. Colin and Bronwyn were now teens too, but Erin had paved the way and I was bit more prepared, as were they. It wasn't always smooth, but there was integrity in the overall operation. I felt, at long last, that my life was working.

# CHAPTER 10

## PACIFIC PALISADES
## HIGH SCHOOL GRADUATION 1988

On the bright Sunday morning of the weekend before the class of 1988 was set to graduate from "Pali," Pacific Palisades High School, Erin and I set out on a mission to find her a graduation outfit in the hip shops in Venice. I knew I wasn't invited along for my fashion advice, but I looked forward to spending the day with my rebellious eldest, who had mostly avoided me for the last four years.

During graduation week, even more parties than usual were in full swing—on the beach, in the parks, at the carousel on Santa Monica Pier, at various homes. My daughter and her friends seemed to be living the beach-blanket-bingo life I had dreamed of as I watched Annette Funicello and Sandra Dee romp around in bikinis on the below-zero Saturdays when I sneaked into the movies in Wisconsin as a teenager.

As usual, I was jockeying between court and kids. In trial

on an age-discrimination case in federal court in San Jose, I was traveling back and forth between San Jose and Los Angeles on weekends. With the jury out, however, and the court taking a recess to allow the defense attorney to attend his son's graduation, I didn't have to return until Wednesday morning.

My client, a sixty-eight-year-old Ukrainian survivor of both the Nazis and Stalin's KGB, had devoted his life to this company and secured several patented pharmaceuticals for them. He had been sent to Europe on expatriate assignment, where he'd established a wildly successful operation for the company. Then, during a mid-1980s takeover and layoff, Mr. S. refused to "take a package" and quit—and the company forced him out with false charges of embezzlement by invoking an arcane tax equalization scheme where expatriate employees, who were paid part foreign currency and part US currency, were required to file US tax returns. Those returns generated refunds, which they then turned over to the company. Mr. S. was ambushed by a battery of Philadelphia lawyers that descended upon his office when he refused to play this game, and fired him then and there. He wept on the stand when answering opposing counsel's questions about the confrontation. "I have been interrogated by the Gestapo and the KGB," he said, "and this was worse." His testimony made some jurors cry.

With closing arguments complete, the weekend was more relaxed than previous weekends had been, filled as they were with preparation of testimony, motions, and arguments. My days now started with yoga inversions, meditation, and laps in the pool of the hotel where I was staying. Nights were spent reviewing evidence, meeting with witnesses, and long shoulder stands on the floor of my hotel room to calm myself when I was ready to jump out of my skin. Now, after weeks of trial, what I fantasized as "a normal woman's life" seemed within reach.

We ran into Teak, willowy and beautiful, with long, sun-streaked hair, in a beachy store near 72 Market Street. She was wandering through the wall-to-wall racks of summery slacks and blouses before meeting her dad for brunch. I asked her what she was going to wear for graduation and she flashed a smile. "I'm not sure. I think . . . like . . . a white suit." There was something especially sweet and even melancholy about her. After a few minutes of small talk, she gave me a big hug and kissed Erin and left. Erin tried on several outfits and finally decided on white Gypsy pants and a white embroidered top, which were lovely and light. We headed off for our Govinda's lunch, vegetarian food I was learning to like as a change from my routine of court cafeteria and hotel food.

*   *   *

At six o'clock on Wednesday morning, June 22, with the radio in my beaten-up old blue Mercedes set on the local news channel, I drove to LAX for my flight to San Jose. I replayed in my head colorful courtroom scenes from the trial to get back into my Joan of Arc character. My first witness to take the stand, a young man who had left his position as vice president to protest the cruel treatment of my client, had brought the tanned and carefully coiffed Mr. Gladwell, a partner in the international steamroller law firm of Gibson Dunn and Crutcher, leaping to his feet.

"She didn't tell us she was calling him first," Gladwell protested. "It is customary to call the plaintiff first . . . I need time to get the witness's deposition."

With the jurors staring on in amazement, Judge Williams peered over his glasses and smiled at the defense table piled high with paper, behind which stood at least twenty file storage boxes manned by file clerks and minions of paralegals.

With all the judicial sarcasm he could muster, Judge Williams responded, "Mr. Gladwell, she doesn't have to tell you what she is going to do. Why don't you just send one of your spear carriers to get the transcript?"

*Bull's-eye*, I thought, *Goliath gets it right between the eyes!* The momentum was all ours. Did I dare think we had the jury with us on a big one here?

On the commute to the airport, my self-congratulatory daydreaming was interrupted by a radio news bulletin that an unidentified young woman's body had been found in the Topa Building on Sunset Boulevard in Pacific Palisades. I felt a chill. The details were sketchy. She'd been found beaten and shot to death in the second-floor women's restroom in the two-story gated office complex. A security guard had found her body.

Things like that don't happen in the Palisades, an affluent enclave on the bluffs overlooking the Pacific. There are security guards everywhere. Armed guards. The news rattled me, and it added to my jitters about the pending jury decision.

I paced the hallways of the courthouse all morning with my client. Around noon we had our verdict: $3,326,000. *Justice is alive*, I thought. I always think that when I win, but the vindication of my client meant the world to him and his family, and the award included both back pay and front pay, lost wages past and future. After a brief hallway caucus with the adjourned panel, I invited all of them, and my opponents, to have a drink across the street at the Fairmont Hotel bar. This was one way to keep an eye on the defense lawyers, who were trolling among the jurors for evidence to overturn the verdict. It was always a tug of war to corral the panel after a verdict. The defense would try in post-trial motions to set aside the verdict, but with this panel there was little chance. Our jurors were highly educated and conscientious, and they'd seen through the defense case.

After only a few moments with the jurors at the bar, I felt sure our verdict was safe. One woman, the jury foreperson, said Mr. Gladwell looked to her like "a divorced tennis player."

Another woman on the jury was an artist and had sketched numerous scenes during the proceedings, which she gave me as a gift. The drawings were her way of taking notes during the trial. I was touched by the gesture, especially as her pen was kind to me. I love courtroom art because, unlike photos or even live television, it captures and highlights particular moments of high drama, focusing on the face-offs between lawyers and witnesses, as well as judges, all through the eyes of a trained observer. Though not official courtroom art, these were great.

On the plane ride home from San Jose late in the afternoon, I was really flying high. Although I had, as usual, gone into debt on the case, I had settled another case through telephone negotiations on a day off during trial that would allow me to pay off the debt. And now, against all odds, I had just won a $3,326,000 verdict against a Fortune 500 company represented by an international law firm in front of a conservative federal judge and a unanimous jury.

\* \* \*

I phoned home as soon as I got back to LAX. Colin and I were verbally high-fiving my first multimillion-dollar trial victory when he whispered, "Erin is crying. Teak's dead . . . Teak's dead." I could hear her wailing.

Erin got on the phone, sobbing, "Teak's dead. A man shot her."

I tried to calm her, insisting it had to be a mistake. I launched into a million questions, an obnoxious defense mechanism of mine that gears up when things get out of control. "How do you know it's Teak? There has to be a mistake."

"Jill just called and said, 'You're going to hear the worst thing you ever heard . . .'"

I sank like a rock to the floor, realizing that Teak had to be the young woman from the early-morning news bulletin. I became frantic to get home, fearing a killer was loose in our neighborhood.

When I got to our house and found no one there, I raced the few blocks to Teak's house and found the house bursting with grieving, lost teens. Jackie, Teak's beautiful and graceful mom, silently wandered around the kitchen, tears streaming down her face. She washed and dried a serving bowl, putting it away in the cabinet under the counter where it belonged, a mother clawing to hold on to a world that was slipping away, trying to put things back in order. I didn't know her well—just as the mother of my daughter's close friend. We walked very different paths: hers the LA entertainment scene, mine the chaotic and singularly unglamorous one of a single mom always struggling to pay the mortgage and my kids' tuition. I stood there helpless, desperately wanting to do something, anything, to ease her pain, knowing there was nothing anyone could do, then or ever.

The grief of a murder victim's mother defies description—except, perhaps, through art. Michelangelo's *Pietà* in Saint Peter's Basilica in Vatican City, a sculpture of Mary lovingly holding the body of her slain son, comes to mind. Her family had identified Teak from crime scene photographs, carefully cropped to shield her from the full carnage and violation Teak had suffered. But nothing could spare her. The photo showed her beautiful child lying in a pool of blood, wearing the pink blouse she was wearing when Jackie last saw her, the night before, on the Santa Monica pier at the carousel. Teak and her friends had been celebrating Teak's eighteenth birthday as well as their impending graduation.

The following afternoon, a huge half-moon hung in the Southern California sky over a gathering of souls seeking comfort in each other and God. The stadium of Palisades High School, a national cinematic symbol of high school hedonism, was the setting for a mass meditation. Teak's family sat in the front row of a makeshift funerary stage. A woman led the emotionally exhausted assemblage in a visualization of colored light flowing into and out of our bodies—healing energy, she called it. As I put my head back and looked up I saw Teak's absence symbolized in the half moon bright against the blue sky . . . profound darkness adjoining brilliant light, her presence and absence both palpable in the crowd that day.

The graduation ceremonies had taken place there that morning, and many graduates had worn caps with *We love you, Teak* written on top. The whole place seemed to be aching. Our family graduation picture in front of "Pali," with Erin in her cap and gown, shows the five of us pale and clinging to each other and trying to smile. In all the chaos of those twenty-four hours, ten-year old Seamus, who had stayed overnight at a friend's house, only learned of the murder that morning, when he asked, "Why is everyone crying?"

Colin put his arm around Seamus and told him, "Teak died last night." Seamus huddled in a corner and sank to the ground, crying. He angrily pushed me away when I tried to console him.

Seamus had loved Teak like one more big sister, and she'd adored him right back. She, the glamorous high school beauty, had made him the envy of his friends when she called out, "Hey, Seamus!" from her red Jeep as she zipped down Montana Avenue. Seamus was proud of her attention and had let his friends know it, hollering back, "Hey, Teak!"

Nothing in my life up to that time had prepared me to mother a family through such terror and loss, and I stumbled blindly a good deal of the time. All five of us spent that night in my bed, hugging each other and talking until it was nearly dawn, afraid to close our eyes, wondering when the police would identify the killer. At that point there were only rumors, and no one had been arrested.

I had been focused on Erin's loss of her friend, but that night I realized I had overlooked how real and painful the trauma was for the other kids, each of whom had his or her own relationship with Teak, and each of whom felt the loss of a virtual sister. Her bike still leaned against our back garden wall. Colin, fourteen, and Bronwyn, thirteen, had watched the TV in horror as the coroner wheeled the covered gurney from the murder scene the day it happened. Then, the announcer said the body "was still unidentified," but now they knew it had been Teak on that gurney. Some evil force had reached into the innocence of our family and yanked out a chunk.

Word spread that a security guard employed by Mac-Guard had been arrested late the afternoon of graduation day. He was the one who had "found" Teak's body. MacGuard was one of the early armed-security services to proliferate in affluent neighborhoods. Pacific Palisades, like many other such communities, was paying big money "to feel safe." Behind that illusion of safety, however, was the reality that private security services brought into these unsuspecting neighborhoods armed and uniformed cop and soldier wannabes who were paid minimum wage and frequently had questionable backgrounds. Some guard candidates, I soon learned, actually brought personally purchased handcuffs and billy clubs to their job interviews. Only the most cursory criminal background check was run on them.

On the day of Teak's memorial, when a passing MacGuard Patrol car broke down in front of the Lake Shrine and Self Realization Fellowship Center, where the service was just ending, several boys had to be restrained from going after the hapless driver.

A few months later, Erin and several other girls went downtown to the Criminal Courts Building to watch the preliminary hearing for Rodney Garmanian, the man charged with Teak's murder. Knowing the kind of photographic evidence that was going to be displayed, I tried to discourage Erin from going. She ignored me. And after a day staring at the back of the head of the man who had murdered Teak, she begged me to come down to the Criminal Courts Building with her, imploring me, "Teak needs you. There is a famous lawyer defending Garmanian, and he asked us if we wanted his autograph. He wears cowboy boots and yells at the judge."

I told her that the prosecutor, Harvey Giss, was an excellent and experienced lawyer and was no doubt doing a great job. I also told her I couldn't do anything in the case, anyway, pointing out the differences between criminal and civil trials, even when they involved the same events.

"Mom," Erin said again. "Teak needs you. She would want you to be there for her, and I do too."

I told her I would try to get there but that I wouldn't be doing anything but watching; still, she insisted, "Teak needs you."

It made no sense that the defense of a $6-per-hour security guard was being handled by a big-shot lawyer, and that he was putting on a defense at the preliminary hearing in a murder case. Most defendants avoid showing their hand and just sit back and use cross examination to shoot holes in the case put on by the district attorney. I also knew from experience what ugly things lay ahead, including hideous crime scene photos of Erin's sweet friend. I cleared my case calendar.

\*　　\*　　\*

When I went with Erin to court the next morning, Melvin Belli, known for years as the King of Torts for his antics and wins in big civil cases, was strutting about the courtroom and calling witness after witness, subpoenaing guards and managers of MacGuard. Criminal cases were not his thing, and yet here he was, preening for the press and the public at a preliminary hearing.

I found Jackie, Teak's mom, sitting in the first row of the gallery alone, separated from her daughter's killer by no more than twenty feet. I took a seat next to her.

By the end of that first day, I found myself pulled into an ugly mystery. One guard after another took the stand to testify, all of them nervous and represented by lawyers. It started to look to me like a cover-up by the guard company. Guns had been switched in the patrol station early in the morning after the body was found. The patrol car Garmanian had been driving was on its way to the carwash when homicide investigators intercepted it.

The managers were being evasive. Within days of the murder, the owner of MacGuard hired and paid $50,000 to Burson-Marstellar, a global public relations firm known for doing damage control. Numerous puff pieces suddenly appeared in local papers lauding the owner of MacGuard. Much was made of the alcohol and cocaine in Teak's blood, and of the fact that she was young, beautiful, and privileged. They blamed her for her own death—never mind that she died of three point-blank gunshots.

I took copious notes over the next ten days, at the end of which I sat with Jackie, doing my best to figure out what was going on and why. I also shared with her my opinion that there seemed to be more to the story.

Garmanian's manager had switched guns with Garmanian when he returned to the station. In addition, dispatch tapes had long erasures for the time period right after the body was found and before Teak was identified as the victim. The role the guard company had played in the whole thing became more troubling with each bit of testimony.

At the end of the preliminary hearing, during which the court had to decide if there was enough evidence of the defendant's guilt to send him to trial, Garmanian was bound over for trial—but, as it turned out, would not go to trial for two years. Meanwhile, the district attorney's office expressed no intention to pursue charges for the possible cover-up by the guard company; they figured they had the killer, and that was enough. The civil courts offered the only other avenue of redress.

I advised the family they could bring a civil case immediately and launch broad discovery through depositions and production of documents that went beyond whether Garmanian was the killer. Why was he working as an armed guard? What was his background? What did or should MacGuard have done before hiring him, and had he been properly supervised? Such a suit should be brought, I informed them, before memories faded and witnesses disappeared. Other lawyers, pursuant to common wisdom, advised the family to delay a civil case until after a conviction in the criminal case, because it would be easier to win then.

The conventional wisdom was fine if the only object was a criminal conviction of Garmanian, followed by a quick financial settlement with the guard company. But it was not about money for Teak's family. They wanted accountability.

Within a few weeks of the preliminary hearing, we filed the civil case and launched discovery, demanding all pertinent company records, including access to the dispatch tapes from both the morning of the murder and the night before.

I was soon contacted by a young woman named Stephanie who, in the weeks before Teak's murder, had been stalked by Garmanian at a house in the Palisades where she was house sitting. Stephanie had called MacGuard upon hearing sounds in the bushes outside the house. Each of three times, Garmanian was the guard who had responded, and he'd started to give her the creeps. She called 911 in terror one night when she heard the doggie door flap and then heard movement in the kitchen; the dog, a young puppy, was with her in the bedroom—so who had just come through the door? On the 911 tape, Stephanie was shaking so badly you could hear the headboard of her bed banging against the wall as she spoke. She felt sure it was Garmanian. The next morning she and her mother went to MacGuard to report their concerns and to insist Garmanian be kept away.

Just a few days later, Stephanie told me that early on the morning of the murder, someone from MacGuard had phoned her and seemed surprised when she answered. They told her the reason for the call was to let her know that they had followed up on her complaint and that Garmanian would be moved to another office.

This call was not on the tape. I decided it was MacGuard's effort to determine if the victim was Stephanie.

Then, out of the blue, I received a phone call from a notorious private investigator.

"This is Anthony Pellicano and I can give you information you can take to the bank," the Chicago tough-guy voice said. "Do you know who I am?" he added.

"Yes, you're the tape expert from the DeLorean case a few years back, right?"

"Yeah," he said, suitably impressed that I recognized what would these days be known as his street cred.

"I can help you on your case with the kid," he said, and I had a feeling he had to be talking about the Teak Dyer wrongful death case. I was creeped out to think of what Pellicano might know about the erasures on the dispatch tapes. But he had been working for a lawyer my clients had consulted before hiring me, so he couldn't have had anything to do with it, I told myself.

I have since learned through wild courtroom testimony that Pellicano frequently worked both sides of a case, and he looked for high-profile cases. But I knew nothing of that at the time.

"You know, she wasn't exactly Rebecca of Sunnybrook Farm," Pellicano said. "They got somethin' on your kid."

My guardian angels sat up straight. The phone felt slimy in my hand. I didn't want this guy anywhere near my clients or me. But I tried to sound thoughtful and professional as I ended the conversation. "I'll talk to my clients but they are not likely to want your services," I said. "We're trying to keep this low profile because it is so painful for her parents."

He called back several more times trying to hustle the case. It had begun receiving national coverage after Garmanian tried, in a bizarre phone call from the jail, to put out a contract on the district attorney, the judge, and the investigator on his criminal case.

I finally told Pellicano, politely, "We have decided we don't need your services."

Pellicano started screaming: "Who the hell do you think you are? I'm fucking Anthony Pellicano."

"Yes, I understand."

Then he spat out, "You'll be sorry," and hung up.

I found myself shaking as I hung up the phone. It was, I learned later, with good reason. He is now in prison for explosives, threats to reporters and witnesses, and illegal wiretapping for and against the biggest attorney names in Los Angeles.

We hired a real expert.

Within hours, Gavin de Becker discovered that Garmanian

had committed a similar attack in a women's bathroom several years earlier in a Chicago office building while working for Pinkerton, the oldest private security guard company in the country, which provided security for the office building,. That victim was an undocumented Polish immigrant, a cleaning woman who narrowly escaped with strangle marks on her neck. MacGuard knew or should have known this and not hired Garmanian.

Jackie sat beside me, unflinching, at every deposition, looking into the eyes of each witness, almost daring them to lie. Many squirmed and tried to avoid her gaze, which seemed to have roughly the effect of truth serum. After months full of deposition and document discovery, the case was sent to trial in Santa Monica before Judge Richard Harris. On a Friday afternoon at the end of the first week of trial, Judge Harris called the attorneys into chambers. The evidence included the dispatch tape call from Garmanian, his sickening voice echoing off the tile walls of the murder scene, as he "phoned in" his discovery of Teak's body. It also included the bloody pink blouse with the bullet hole in it and the crime scene photographs.

Judge Harris, a seasoned trial court judge who didn't hesitate to put pressure on attorneys, turned to defense counsel and asked, "Who is the adjuster on the case? Has the carrier offered the policy limits?"

The answer he got from defense counsel did not sit well with him. "Your Honor, they are in Arizona and we can reach them by phone if we need them. We don't believe there is liability here, so policy limits aren't important."

"I think we see this case differently. What are the limits?"

"One million dollars, Your Honor."

"Good. Where is your adjuster?"

When he was told that not even an adjuster from the Arizona-based insurance carrier was in court, he was furious. "On

Monday morning, I want you back here with full authority to settle this case for the policy limits or have the president of the insurance company here to explain why not."

He adjourned for the weekend.

\*   \*   \*

First thing Monday morning, Judge Harris called me into chambers alone.

"Peggy, the carrier has the full $1 million policy limit this morning."

Now it was my turn to face judicial wrath. Standing just inside Judge Harris's chambers, as if I were in a hurry, I said, "I'll go speak to my clients about it, but I don't think they will take it. They want a jury verdict, and they don't care about the money."

With an unyielding, grandfatherly voice, Judge Harris, who had reined in probably thousands of trial lawyers over the years and could spot a reckless one, said firmly, "Sit down, Peggy." And so I did. "Listen to me carefully. You are not going to just go out there and 'offer' this to your clients. It is a deal. You are going to tell them to take it. You cannot have them sit through what comes next here. In the criminal case, maybe, but not here. Bring them to me. I want to talk to them."

A judge cannot order a lawyer or litigant to settle a case, of course; but that's not what Judge Harris was doing. He was just trying to do the best thing for my clients and, in the bargain, save me from myself. Judge Harris could see that I couldn't let go, didn't want to stop until I had someone's head on a platter. I had become a trial machine. I had a score to settle (which I had made pretty clear in my opening statement as I insisted, "Teak's spirit will guide you through the evidence to determine what happened. Only you, the jury, can impose full accountability on the company that recklessly put a murderer into our neighbor-hood where he could prey upon our daughters").

Sputtering "but, but, but . . ." I went to get my clients, still trying to figure out how I could get around Judge Harris. We talked for a bit outside the courtroom—a trailer, actually, that had been set up as a courtroom to serve the overcrowded and dilapidated Santa Monica courthouse. Even in this flimsy setup, where the usual auspiciousness of a court with marble halls and elevated benches was not in view, and where the green-carpeted plywood floorboards creaked underfoot, it was impossible not to feel the power of the law to render justice. This was especially so in Judge Harris's courtroom.

I explained to Jackie and Rod what the judge had told me. They looked surprised that we were even discussing settlement. Like me, they did not want to stop this train we were on. After a very brief conversation, we headed back into chambers.

Thank God Jackie and Rod listened as Judge Harris explained, "Even if you win, there could be appeals and this might go on forever. Stopping now would be a total victory. It is hard to imagine that any verdict will be higher than this—but, more important, you can put this behind you. I know you want a public record, so we can do a settlement and judgment, which is the same as a verdict."

I was no match for Judge Harris, and I saw that he was doing everything in his power to give my clients what they needed: accountability. His timing was impeccable, too, because Teak's parents had testified and had their day in court—some-thing wounded people really need in order to start healing.

It would not be the typical, confidential, sweeping-it-under-the-rug settlement. Judge Harris entered a stipulated judgment in the amount of $1 million, to be recorded and paid immediately, and there would be a published judgment identical to what would have happened with a verdict. Conventional wisdom then held that the economic value of the life of an eighteen-year-old, still economically dependent upon her parents, was in the range of $300,000. This judgment said so much more. We didn't know it then, but MacGuard would go out of business soon after—and, after Jackie and our security expert, Gavin de Becker, testified before the California Legislature, a law was passed requiring more stringent regulations for security guards.

# CHAPTER 11

# WORKING ON THE RAILROAD

# AND JUMPING HURDLES

It was summer 1992. Over the past several months, the streets of Los Angeles had been the stage of a compelling drama. The defining moment was the nationally televised beating of white truck driver Reginald Denny, pulled from his big rig by rioters after six white Los Angeles cops were acquitted in the clubbing, a year earlier, of black motorist Rodney King. King's beating, captured on videotape by a passerby and played on television over and over for the following year, had shocked and horrified the world—and the acquittal of the cops by an all-white jury had set the black community off like a spark to tinder. The riots had gone on for days, resulting in more than fifty deaths and widespread burning and looting.

I was in trial in federal court in downtown Los Angeles on a gross sexual harassment case against Southern Pacific Railroad. On my way to court each morning around 7 A.M., I drove by a homeless encampment where people congregated on the sidewalk around a makeshift stove, coffee brewing in a battered old tin pot—the kind you see in westerns when the cowboys gather around the campfire.

One morning I wondered, fleetingly, if I were the only "suit" who sometimes envied the lives I passed on the way to work. It was 7 A.M., and the little village of houses cobbled together from cardboard boxes, in various stages of destruction and reconstruction, was coming to life. Some members of the encampment were just getting up; others milled around in animated conversation, sipping coffee. Occasionally, I forgot the outrage of such poverty and homelessness in this rich city of ours. I imagined camaraderie among these urban villagers— something along the lines of "we're all in this together." There didn't seem to be any rush to get anywhere or do anything. *They are not only homeless*, I thought, *but also mortgage-less*. I quickly snapped back to realizing the good fortune I had in my own life and told myself to stop the mental whining. I was fortunate beyond anything I could have imagined as a child growing up in my small town in Wisconsin. I was a Los Angeles trial lawyer, and I was doing exciting things.

I had been slugging it out in a male-dominated profession for nearly twenty years, had four great kids, and was frequently told, "You have it all." I did have a very blessed and vibrant life, albeit as a single mother with a very irregular paycheck. I was doing exactly what I wanted to do: taking on the bad guys to challenge unfairness and gender bias in the system, including race, pregnancy, promotions, and wage discrimination, and, of course, sexual harassment. The 1991 Senate confirmation hearings for Clarence Thomas to the US Supreme Court forced upon our public consciousness the glaring gender-based cultural disconnect on sexual harassment in the workplace. Afterward, women who before had been too ashamed to come forward to complain found the courage to bring such cases into the courts, and I got very busy. It was a whole new day for women, and we were finally demanding equality in the workplace.

At the same time, I was in the midst of dealing with crushing high school and college tuition obligations for four kids, had just refinanced my house for the second time in two years, and was in credit card debt up to my eyeballs, as I always was by the time I was in trial on a contingency case like the one I was trying that day. I must have been cracking under the pressure, because I also envied the woman I saw at the top of a telephone pole on Pacific Coast Highway that morning. I smiled when I saw her at the top of the pole—visible proof that women could do the heavy duty and high-paying jobs from which they had historically been excluded. Based on my professional experience, I assumed she had run a gauntlet of sexual harassment as she worked her way to that spot atop the pole. Nevertheless, I thought to myself, that woman would do her work, actually fix something, and go home, the job done. My trial, on the other hand, could turn into motions, appeals, and retrials, and go on forever.

As I headed to court that day, I saw reminders of the riots all around, and with my own twisted logic, instead of seeing destruction and hopelessness, I saw the possibilities in people taking to the streets to demonstrate against social grievances. Most people I knew were terrified by the riots. My opponent on the case in trial had even refused to travel out of LAX for depositions of the two highly regarded sexual harassment experts I hired to testify. Judge Kenner, on the defendant's request, had ordered that the depositions be taken during the afternoons after the day in trial. It made for a very long day, as we were required to have witnesses on the stand in the courtroom by 8 A.M.

Blackened palms like burned-out torches stood over the

street, maimed survivors of the riots. Someone had even tried to throw a trash can through the beautiful glass doors of the federal courthouse, cracking the thick security glass. On this morning, however, the streets were quiet as I pulled into the parking lot a few blocks from the courthouse.

Dressed in my dark blue, pinstripe skirt suit, white silk blouse, and high heels, I heaved boxes of documents and trial books from my trunk onto a trolley, which I then dragged across the freeway overpass, down the block, and into the federal courthouse. I was really good at this, if not graceful. Once inside, each box had to be lifted off the trolley, hoisted onto the conveyor belt that ran them through the metal detector, and then put back onto the trolley for the elevator ride up to the courtroom, where I had to repeat the unloading process. As I passed through the screener alongside the conveyor belt, the buzzer went off and the guard gestured for me to go back, remove my shoes and belt, and go through again. I complied, patting my pockets for any other possible offending item and dropping my portable Dictaphone and calculator into the plastic bowl the guard dug through. I knew the telephone repairwoman wasn't going through all this just to get to work.

Finally, I rearranged my traveling show and headed up to the courtroom.

Marilyn, my client, alleged that she had left her job at Southern Pacific Railroad after her boss, Mr. Fitzgerald, masturbated on her desk. This peculiar act was shocking enough that people initially refused to believe it. But it got crazier. His defense at trial was that it was consensual oral copulation, part of an ongoing affair. The jury would have to decide: oral copulation or masturbation.

To make my case, I would have to use raw and explicit language. I was trying to get Judge Kenner to allow the shocking testimony of another former employee who had been hospitalized for a nervous breakdown after Fitzgerald sexually taunted him in front of his male co-workers. After that employee filed a lawsuit against the railroad several years earlier, Fitzgerald had reportedly driven him around the rail yard in his truck, pushing his head down into his lap and calling out, "He's sucking my dick." The employee had been ostracized and pelted with food in the lunchroom.

I wanted to show both a pattern of sexual harassment by Fitzgerald, and that the employer knew about it. I needed to convince Judge Kenner that this was in fact sexual harassment even though both perpetrator and victim were men, something not yet recognized in the case law. These were the early days of sexual harassment cases and there had not yet been a legal determination that men could also be harassed by male bosses. During earlier motion hearings he had ruled against me when I contended the behavior demonstrated a pattern and practice—Fitzgerald using sex to humiliate complaining employees—and that Southern Pacific knew or should have known about it. But sexual harassment is defined as the abuse of power using sex, end of story. This seemed the perfect case to illustrate that harassment could happen to anyone.

In his opening statement, the defense counsel had opened the door for this evidence, asserting that Fitzgerald had never sexually harassed anyone. In making such a broad assertion, he was relying on the court ruling denying my motion to allow testimony from the male employee who had been so grossly humiliated. However, if arguments or evidence develop during a trial, a new and different ruling may be warranted. Once my opponent asserted to the jury that Fitzgerald had never sexually harassed anyone, I had the right to disprove that assertion. He had set the stage for the highly inflammatory testimony the judge had previously precluded.

Judge Kenner was a formal man who in motion hearings a few months earlier had dubbed masturbation "this solo business" and nearly choked when uttering the phrase "oral copulation." The earlier hearings had been the beginning of the inevitable fight over what evidence could be presented to the jury at trial, and because it was a sexual harassment case, my word choice was, necessarily, explicit. The judge had winced when I'd talked about masturbation, oral copulation, suspicious stains on slipcovers, vibrators, and polka dot panties. But I'd pressed on—I had to familiarize our judge with just what was going to be heard in this case. As if possessed I then blurted, "Fitzgerald was the head honcho. He used plaintiff to get the lay of the land, and then brought her to her knees."

I'd enlisted Colin to help me with witness management—always a tricky proposition in federal court, where judges were short on patience. I was relying upon my son to deliver the terrified former employee of Southern Pacific—the man from the pickup truck—to the stand.

I unloaded my trolley of file boxes that held our deposition transcripts, trial notebooks, and other evidence, and placed them underneath my counsel table. Then I went into the hall to find the psychiatrist hired by one of my client's original attorneys, who had opined in deposition that Fitzgerald was a sexual predator. I had not yet met her, but knew her from her television persona as a forensic psychiatrist. Her evaluation in this case, however, was based solely on depositions of the parties, without any actual examinations. She was far from being a bulletproof expert, and as such was someone I would not have chosen if I'd had the case from the beginning. But her deposition, which had been taken long before I came on the case, was favorable to my client, and since one never knows what experts the court will allow to render expert testimony, I hadn't eliminated her.

When I found her, she was wandering the empty halls eating a Hershey bar, a *People* magazine tucked under her arm. I introduced myself, and my amusement turned to alarm when she opened her mouth and said through chocolate sludge, "I watched the video again last night. I think they were having an affair."

She'd changed her opinion without notifying anyone? I could not imagine putting this loose cannon on the stand.

Since I'd taken on this case three months earlier, it had been a whirlwind of ups and downs. But I had been moved by my client's suffering, so I'd dived in. I felt as if I was truly taking on *the man*.

Just the day before, the defense lawyer had made a passionate motion to preclude the psychiatrist from testifying. Now, faced with her change of heart, I decided to propose we compromise to "stipulated testimony"—a bland factual recitation of what she intended to testify to, read by one of the lawyers. If I could get them to agree, and I thought I could, we would be spared her live testimony and there would, blessedly, be no cross-examination.

"Dr. Jones, stay right here and relax with your magazine," I told her. "I'll come get you for your testimony."

"I can't stay any longer than this morning."

"Oh, don't worry. I won't keep you beyond noon. We might not even need you to testify." I suggested we take the elevator up one floor and sit and talk a bit. I stashed her up there, in a place where she was not likely to run across my opponent, and told her I would come back to get her only if and when she was needed. I hoped I would be able to send her home without having her appear in court.

My mind racing, I sprinted down the escalator to start my court day. Once there, I was focused and ready for battle. There is something sacred about a courtroom, especially a federal courtroom. I was still as in awe of it as I had been of church as a child. I couldn't imagine any juror not taking his or her job seriously in this somber place, where the elevated bench stood before a backdrop of the seal of the United States of America and was flanked by the US and California flags.

"Peggy, look at the lotuses around the jury box," Marilyn had whispered on the first day. "I think that's good luck for us." Sure enough, lotuses were carved into the exquisite wood paneling just below the railing around the jury box. I wondered about the New Deal artisan who'd labored there, and whether this ancient symbol of the heart was meant to signify that the jury is the heart of our court system. Marilyn and I closed our eyes and visualized the positive effect this garland of lotuses might have on our jury panel.

At this point our case had been going well and I felt it was about to get even better. We were about a week into trial, and I was probably going to cross-examine Fitzgerald. I could hardly wait. But everything depended upon the psychiatrist's testimony and on whether the court would allow the testimony of the male employee Fitzgerald had harassed. The motion to allow it was going to be heard, yet again, today.

I thought excitedly of the old documents I had found the night before in some boxes I inherited when I took on the case—documents that contradicted and discredited the defendant. Mr. Fitzgerald had denied under oath several years earlier that he'd had any sexual relationship with my client, who had been represented by different lawyers at the time. Now, in trial, Fitzgerald was asserting that they had been involved in a consensual affair. From what I could discern, either the defense had lost track of those old documents, or they assumed I didn't know about them because I was so new to the case. I would have to wait until Fitzgerald was on the stand to nail him with his lies. I felt like a kid on Christmas Eve.

After I stated in open court what the former employee would say during his testimony, the judge nearly spat out his ruling: "This 'suck my dick' stuff is the same thing he said to Moss. It comes in." I saw the light go on in his eyes; he suddenly and viscerally understood sexual harassment. It wasn't sex. It was abuse of power *using* sex. This was going to be a very big day. The abused former employee would get to take the stand.

My opponent and I entered into a stipulation as to what the psychiatrist's expert testimony would be. She wouldn't testify now, thank God. I loved that the boys on the other side thought they had won the point. The match was just starting.

Next the diminutive former employee, his fear palpable, entered the courtroom. His eyes looking anywhere but at Fitzgerald, the terrified shell of a man followed Colin to the witness stand.

As I watched the graceful young man my son now was, I remembered how he had loved the courtroom as a little boy. When he was six, he had stood holding my hand as both the judge and my opposing counsel introduced themselves to him. Always certain thereafter that I could put things right with the world, he'd never missed a chance to come to court to observe and help.

Colin returned to his seat. Eyes downcast, the former employee told his story, withstanding aggressive cross-examination from the other side—something that just made him more sympathetic to the jury. The railroad's lawyers came off like bullies who couldn't resist beating him up again. They played right into my hands.

After the pummeling, the judge turned to the witness and said, "You are excused."

"Can I talk to Peggy first?" he asked.

Judge Kenner gestured for me to approach the stand. As I walked slowly around counsel table, past the jury, and up the five or six steps to the witness stand, I wondered what on earth

131

he was going to say, and why the judge was allowing it. The view from up there was far more intimidating. As I leaned in, the former employee whispered, "I thought you were going to ask me everything."

"Didn't you tell us everything?" I asked.

"No."

I returned to the podium. "Your honor, may I reopen my direct of this witness?" I asked.

"Yes, you may," Judge Kenner said. "Please proceed."

"Is there something you need to add to or change about your testimony?" I asked the witness, assuming he felt the need to correct something he'd already stated.

Suddenly animated, the witness pointed at Fitzgerald and cried, "He's a dog. He's a monster. He put me in the hospital with a nervous breakdown, shock treatments, ruined my family and my life . . ."

Before I could formulate a response to this blindside, which I had to do because I knew I would be accused of sandbagging this testimony for dramatic impact, Fitzgerald exploded to his feet and lunged almost over the counsel table, knocking over a water pitcher. His lawyer grabbed him and implored the judge to declare a mistrial.

Judge Kenner looked stunned but denied the motion. This drama was unquestionably genuine and spontaneous—and Fitzgerald had shown his colors. He was one scary fellow, and the whole courtroom felt it. The former employee had gotten the chance to say what he needed to say to restore his self-respect, it seemed, because all five foot four of him walked tall out of the courtroom.

In a hurried move to rehabilitate the defendant, opposing counsel put Fitzgerald on the stand. Predictably, he denied the former employee's accusations and then, in a teary confession, said he'd had an affair with my client and was devastated to have hurt his wife and family. I did not interrupt this melodrama with a single objection. I let it sink in. I had him. Cross-examination would be fun. I started in.

"So, Mr. Fitzgerald, you told your wife about your affair?"

"Yes."

"You told her you were sorry?"

"Yes."

"Is your wife in the courtroom?"

"No."

"But she knows you are here in trial, right?"

"No."

This came as a surprise to me, though I was sure he was lying about having confessed his infidelity to her. I knew she wouldn't be in the courtroom, because now that Fitzgerald had testified about a privileged conversation with his wife I could call her as a hostile witness, and I would have great latitude in questioning. But this could be gold, so I proceeded across the equivalent of hot coals, very softly.

"Where do you tell her you are going in the morning?"

"To work."

Bingo. Fitzgerald had just admitted to lying to his wife every morning. Chances were he was hiding the whole thing from her. I had to underline it for the jury.

"So, every morning, before you come to court and swear to tell the truth, you lie to your wife?"

*Objection, objection, objection!*

*Overruled!*

I just bloodied the defendant in a way I had not even planned. I couldn't blow it now. I proceeded very slowly, very clearly, reading directly from discovery documents I handed to the jury to pass around after the testimony.

"Mr. Fitzgerald, you did, however, apologize to her for your infidelity?"

"Yes."

"I'm showing you your statement in written answers to Requests for Admissions from four years ago, under oath, saying you deny any sexual activity of any kind whatsoever took place between you and Marilyn . . . You see that?"

I waited a beat. The next question was obvious and deadly.

"Were you lying then, or are you lying now?"

I couldn't believe this. It was a lawyer's dream. Even the timing felt orchestrated by the angels. The theme from "Perry Mason" played in my head. The unfolding drama was such that someone went running from the courtroom and said, within earshot of Colin, "It's like TV in there!"

Sometimes I got to be an instrument of justice, and this was one of those times. I couldn't help wondering if even Mrs. Fitzgerald wouldn't have enjoyed seeing her husband get nailed for this.

Near the end of trial, Judge Kenner ordered counsel to stay after court to work on jury instructions—but when the time came, the silver-haired senior partner was nowhere in sight. He had addressed me as "little girl" during the trial, and his walk was what you'd call a swagger—intended to let the jury know he was in charge. He'd also spent the last several days entertaining the judge with jock talk during chambers conferences, a not-uncommon move in such circles; it was intended to sideline the "little girl" in the room. Older male lawyers, for whom female lawyers were a relatively new phenomenon, were sometimes overt in their tactics to diminish me, and by now I had begun to see it as a sport. I'd learned quickly that what goes on in a judge's chambers can powerfully impact the way a case goes back in the courtroom. It was as intimidating as any boys' club, but to not participate was a tactical default. I had to find a way in.

The first time opposing counsel started schmoozing with the judge, my mind had raced to come up with an entrée. I'd scrambled to come up with my own jock stories. When Judge Kenner mentioned his son had to put in ridiculous hours for football as a freshman in college, I elbowed my way in.

"I know what you mean," I said. "My daughter does the pentathlon on the Yale track team and has really crazy workouts that make it hard to keep up with all the academics."

Judge Kenner raised his eyebrows in surprise and turned his full attention to me. He asked what high school she had attended, looking as if he preferred this personal kind of sports talk. Two chairs over, the silver fox squirmed. When I said Brentwood, Judge Kenner smiled and pointed out that his son's baseball team had beaten Brentwood. Now it was the other lawyer's turn out in left field.

Ron, the younger partner, and I were both exhausted but went on until late afternoon. He was a decent guy, and I had to confess to him that my kids had observed him in trial and warned me that he was "a good attorney." During our many hours together, like two kids sent to our room for fighting, we found ourselves actually talking, almost bonding. We talked about our families. He had seen my brood come and go from the courtroom, and reported catching Bronwyn napping on one of the benches at the back, red cowboy boots hanging over the end. He had two little boys, and I was stunned to learn that his wife, a lawyer and now stay-at-home mom, was hard at work for Bill Clinton's presidential campaign. I realized then that I operated on knee-jerk stereotypes. As I always tell potential jurors during *voir dire*, we all have prejudices, and the challenge is to not let those prejudices and biases take over.

The following morning we did closing arguments and the judge read the instructions we had agreed on to the jury, telling them how to apply the law to the facts of the case.

Then we stood around the hallway, waiting for a verdict.

I was buoyed when the jury asked for a calculator. They must be at damages already, both my opponents and I realized, because if they hadn't found Southern Pacific liable, there would be no need for a calculator. We had been negotiating ever since the jury entered deliberations, as most lawyers typically do, since one never knows what a jury will do. Both sides usually want to avoid the risk of losing, and also the delays and expense of appeals, which can happen no matter what the verdict. At this point we all want a conclusion, with the plaintiff wanting to get the best amount the defendants will pay, and with the defendants trying to pinpoint the least amount plaintiff will accept. I was feeling very confident at this point and could tell opposing counsel was deeply concerned. They were going back and forth to the phone booth.

In an effort to settle the case before there was a jury verdict, I demanded settlement in the sum of $3 million—significantly less than I argued for the jury to award in damages, but a substantial sum. I tweaked opposing counsel, saying, "If we let this case go through to a jury verdict, I think the verdict here will make the $25 million award last year against Texaco look like small potatoes." My opponents, fearing just that, raised their settlement offer to $2.5 million. Just then the clerk stepped into the hallway holding aloft a thin brown envelope and announced, "There is a verdict." We all froze.

Having developed unbecoming trial lawyer cockiness, I said with all the swagger I could muster, "Let's go take it." Ron implored me to wait for them to make one more call to corporate headquarters. I agreed. He came back with an acceptance of my $3 million demand and we headed into the courtroom. I told the clerk we had a settlement and needed the court reporter to put it into the record. As soon as the court reporter arrived, we were all led into chambers.

Judge Kenner, always inscrutable, sat behind his massive desk and gestured for us to take a seat across from him. The silver fox didn't look at me.

I strived to be formal in federal court. I was wearing my standard conservative blue pinstripe skirt suit with starched white collar, high heels and, as always, my expired wedding ring. Fitting in here was a delicate balance for a woman, requiring a schizophrenic combination of trial lawyer toughness and respectable womanhood. While kicking their asses, I had to appear the finishing school graduate. I had been raised for this moment. There was no jock talk now.

The court reporter set up her machine to record the settlement and, after commending us for reaching a settlement in this hard-fought case, Judge Kenner told me to proceed. I recited it all—deadline for payment and penalties for late payment spelled out, and specifying that the settlement would be entered as a judgment of the court. I wanted it ironclad, with no wiggle room for interpretation. It took about ten minutes to cover it all. I thanked Judge Kenner and started to collect my things, packing up my heavy leather briefcase. The silver fox whispered something to Ron.

I was horrified when opposing counsel insisted we have a look at the verdict form. I did not want to see it, because I was sure I had walked away from millions in settling for the $3 million. We all thought the jury verdict would have been higher than the settlement. The railroad company wanted to know because they believed the jury verdict I passed up would be for an astronomical sum, and they could rub my nose in it.

The judge, one eyebrow raised to look like a question mark, had a look on his face I interpreted, as "Are you sure?" Then he handed the paper across to the three of us. We leaned forward to look at the verdict and we all gasped. The jury award was going to be $250,000, with a finding of punitive damages. This would have required a trial to determine the amount of punitive damages, and while it could have been high (it's based upon the wealth of the defendants), the initial award would not have made that likely. I marveled at this crazy constitutional system.

The jury is essential to this part of the process, even without a formal verdict, and even after a full trial and jury deliberations. Settlement happens only when both sides realize they stand to lose. And this is how the system best serves both sides. It is also why the tort reformers want to eliminate the jury system—to weight the scales of justice to their singular advantage, by, for example, making the losing side pay the attorney fees for the winner or limiting damages awards. The former is designed to intimidate potential plaintiffs from bringing cases, and the latter to limit their access to lawyers. For consumers, it is dangerous to abandon the jury system, as flawed as it is.

I summoned my brood to celebrate over lunch at Ocean Seafood in Santa Monica. Seamus took several buses to get home from the San Fernando Valley, and then skateboarded several miles to the beach to meet us. We celebrated the fact that Erin, Colin, and Bronwyn could all go back to Brooks, NYU, and Yale in the fall, since I could now pay the tuition. We always somehow had what we needed, usually at the last possible moment. Hank, the man in my life, the supportive one I didn't marry, marveled at what seemed to be miracles in my life, saying, "You must do it with mirrors."

Seamus, for whom school had always been a trial, was going into ninth grade and had argued his case for going to boarding school. "Mom, if I go to SaMo"—that's what the local kids called Santa Monica High School—"I'm going to mess up." He had apparently learned some legal concepts by osmosis, because he was giving me what amounted to notice of likely adverse consequences. He was campaigning to go to the school where a friend's unruly boy had gone and done well—where classes were small, and daily skiing, rock climbing, and other survival activities were part of the curriculum. Survival skills and hands-on teaching in small classes with instant consequences would be good for this kid, whose detentions and other disciplines were such a constant that it seemed I spent as much time at his school as he did.

I was about to become an empty nester with kids in schools in four different states. Solvency was not a natural state for me and had never been. This moment was one of the rare times in my life I felt financially secure. And yet I was resisting getting married again, this time to Hank, the most decent man ever to walk into my life. He was there with us, as he always was, if I let him, to celebrate our good fortune and a bright future. As a lawyer he had been my sounding board and much more as I fought my way through this and many other cases, offering great ideas or playing devil's advocate, even telling me jokes in the middle of the night when I couldn't sleep. He could always make me laugh and put things in perspective. Where I was wild and crazy, he was calm and predictable. Where I was profligate and impulsive, he was organized and frugal. But I just couldn't trust myself to do it again.

Colin, playing Clyde to my Bonnie, drove the getaway car when I went downtown one week later to collect the check for $3 million. In 1992, Moss v. Southern Pacific was the highest paid sexual harassment judgment in the country, and I continued attracting more.

# CHAPTER 12

# TWO MOTHERS

# TAKE ON THE BIG GUNS

In 1995, I took on the case of an African American woman investigator in the Los Angeles district attorney's office. She alleged sexual harassment, sex discrimination and race discrimination. Virginia and I bonded as fast friends. Unbeknownst to either of us, our paths had crossed years before: she had been one of the original district attorney investigators on Teak's murder in summer 1988. Many years before, her first job in law enforcement had been a stint working in the women's jail.

When she wanted more professional experience, she moved over to the LA district attorney's office and was the original investigator on the notorious McMartin preschool molestation case. But the case was given to two white male deputies as soon as it got big press and started to pay double overtime.

Still, Virginia was a team player who finally had a good shot at becoming head investigator in the DA's Santa Monica branch—a spot currently held by head investigator Henry Grayson, who doubled as DA Ira Reiner's driver and bodyguard. In addition to squiring the Reiner around town, he carried a gun and provided security for him while he was out of the office. Grayson was able to maintain this cushy job even after a highly publicized debacle that took place in front of Spago one evening: the DA's limousine was stolen . . . with Grayson sitting in it.

Grayson, we eventually concluded, for some reason perceived Virginia's ascendancy as a threat to his own—and when Virginia spurned his persistent sexual advances, he retaliated by accusing her of poor performance. Virginia lodged a complaint against him and was immediately transferred downtown, where, despite twenty years of stellar job performance, she was demoted. The message was clear: "You are not one of us."

Grayson was being personally represented, behind the scenes, by Johnnie Cochran, already something of a celebrity. In the courtroom, Grayson was represented by the Los Angeles County Counsel's Office, but Cochran was there to protect his client's personal interests. Cochran would show up in the first few days of the trial, and either sit in the front row of the courtroom or hang around the defense counsel table so the jury could see him chatting up the DA representatives. On the day he became part of the "Dream Team" defending O.J. Simpson, Cochran phoned the courtroom and the clerk announced, "Johnnie Cochran for Mr. Grayson"—a tactic clearly designed to get the jury's attention and show how important Grayson was.

Groups of DA investigators and office personnel huddled outside the courtroom in the hallway daily, as if the gang-like swagger of these paragons of law enforcement could intimidate or scare us. The game was to get us to drop the case or make some big mistake; we all knew the facts were on our side.

One day, a wild-eyed investigator known as a hothead was called to the stand to testify against Virginia. He walked to the stand slowly, carrying a heavy duffel bag. As he stepped up to the stand, he dropped the bag onto the floor alongside the witness chair and glared at Virginia. The alarm on her face was immediate, and I couldn't understand it. But she got the message loud and clear.

"That bag is full of guns," she whispered to me. "I heard them. He's trying to scare me."

Since the man had nothing relevant to offer in the way of testimony, I took her at her word.

Things escalated. As Virginia sat on the bench outside the courtroom, a man she didn't recognize approached, made eye contact, then reached into a briefcase and clicked the chamber of a gun.

After this latest threat, I alerted the bailiff. This was in the days before metal detectors were installed in all courthouses, and the people threatening us were law enforcement officers.

The bailiff listened, and then set us straight. "You're winning. If you report this to the judge he will call a mistrial, and it will be over. That's what they want you to do. Everyone is watching and rooting for you. Don't stop now. You will never get this far again."

We took her advice. This woman was watching out for us.

In the afternoon, when the judge took the bench, Virginia failed to appear at counsel table. The judge was annoyed. I made a motion for recess and dashed out of the courtroom. I found her in the bathroom, throwing up. She was in distress, terrified by the many threats against her life. Rather than tell the judge, I requested and got a recess for the rest of the afternoon—so that she could recover from a "migraine."

We won Virginia's case after a hotly contested, three-weeklong trial. I cross-examined both District Attorney Reiner and federal Judge Audrey Collins, the first black woman appointed to the federal bench. To Virginia's great distress, Judge Collins, a friend, was called to testify against her. I objected vigorously to Judge Collins being identified as a federal judge when she took the stand because of the potential for bias. What juror would view the testimony of a federal judge as anything but gospel truth? But the trial judge overruled me, saying, "I am not going to have a federal judge appear in my courtroom and not recognize her as such."

The District Attorney's office called Judge Collins to the stand as if trumpeting the arrival of royalty. We all stood in acknowledgment. The testimony was subtle; not dramatic, except for the fact that it was being delivered by a federal judge. Judge Collins, who had been a top deputy in the District Attorney's Office at the time, testified that Virginia was transferred downtown as a routine personnel matter. This implied that Virginia's testimony that her transfer was retaliatory was incorrect. Judge Collins seemed to believe that was the case, and perhaps it was. She wouldn't have lied under oath. But because of the impact of a sitting federal judge taking the stand as a witness, I had to find some way to challenge her testimony . . . without attacking a highly regarded federal judge whom I, too, respected.

As I stood before the jury in closing argument, I felt myself suddenly choked up and groping for words. "While I rejoice in Judge Collins's crossing impossible race and gender barriers, I weep for the political debt she had to pay." I don't know where that came from. It was completely spontaneous, and it was all I said about her testimony.

While their mother's case was pending, Virginia's son, Kelly, and daughter, Erica, had come with her to several back-yard barbecues at my house, where they joined a poolful of kids their age, including Seamus and his friends. I regularly threw parties for clients after winning a case and invited other clients whose cases were pending to show them there was in fact light at the end of the tunnel. Kelly and Erica were the center of Virginia's life. They had attended Saint Monica's Catholic High School, even though they were not Catholic, solely because she wanted to have them near her office in Santa Monica. And children go through a tumult when their mothers are harassed, make a complaint, are retaliated against, or lose their jobs. They go through it all again when the company defends itself by smearing her with the standard "she's-a-nut-and-a-slut defense." I found that bringing together families in various stages of litigation provided a place for defusing the experience. I hoped that was the case for Virginia and her kids.

Virginia's victory at trial changed things for women in law enforcement. When our case started, there were no women above the rank of captain and no women supervisors; now fourteen out of thirty-seven supervisors are black women, five are Lieutenants, two are captains, and the assistant chief of investigators is a black woman. After a long impasse, they started to get promoted through the ranks. Instead of returning to the office she had sued, Virginia launched her own investigation agency. She also became a real estate agent so she could make the extra money needed to send her kids to their first choice colleges.

Kelly ultimately decided to attend Florida A&M University. In late April 2000—near the end of his fourth year in a five-year combined bachelor's/master's in business program, and just after his twenty-second birthday—he was shot to death by street kids trying to rob him. An assistant district attorney who knew I was Virginia's close friend phoned me with the devastating news.

Virginia was an optimistic and resilient woman who had overcome incredible odds and obstacles. She had grown up in

Texas and told me, with no discernible anger or resentment, about attending movies in segregated theaters and having to climb up to the "coloreds only" balcony with her mother. Her mother and she had accepted as God's will the loss of her only brother in a house fire. I wondered how she was going to cope with this, every mother's greatest fear.

A faithful churchgoer, Virginia was immediately embraced by her fellow parishioners, and friends and relatives came from all over. I would see her at her son's funeral.

A few days after I got the call about Kelly, Seamus phoned me from Boston, where he was in his second year at Berklee College of Music: "Mom, my new computer just got stolen with all the programs on it. The cops just left here." After opening his door to a guy he thought he knew because they had shared an occasional marijuana pipe, Seamus had been marched at gunpoint to his ATM to get cash and then, when there was none, back to his apartment.

I held my breath and resisted the urge to cross-examine him.

"He set his gun on my bed and went over to my computer," Seamus continued. "I told him the computer was brand-new and all I had, but that he could take it. He called his friends, who were outside in a car, to ask what to do. After he hung up he picked up his gun and said, 'Get down on the floor and make this easier on both of us.' I told him I wouldn't."

"You what?" I said.

"Mom, I wasn't going to lie down," Seamus explained breathlessly. "I told him, 'You're throwing your life away. You don't have to do this . . . You don't want to do this . . . Your life will be over, too. You'll go to hell.'"

The assailant left with Seamus's new computer, fully loaded with state-of-the-art music composition programs and all of his composition work for the semester.

"He said they'd come back if I called the cops, but I thought I had to call. The cops just left and told me to be careful."

My alarms went off. Seamus was in more danger than he realized, especially if the cops had been seen coming and going from his apartment by the assailant and his crew. I called my secretary, Mary, and asked her to get Seamus out of Boston as quickly as possible. Mary arranged for Seamus to take a taxi to the airport and fly home immediately. I picked him up at dawn. He didn't know it yet, but I was not letting him go back to Boston, not even to retrieve his things. He would, after we wrangled for a bit, finish at Cal Arts. Easygoing California kids at out-of-state colleges seemed to me to be easy targets, and I wanted to get my youngest out of the line of fire.

Seamus and I attended Kelly's funeral together, both of us numb and keenly aware that we had been passed over by the angel of death, as another mother's child had just been taken. Kelly's family and friends filled the church, too familiar with this ritual for their young ages. Virginia and I had joined forces and vanquished a powerful Los Angeles establishment, only to be brought low by the loss of one of our sons, and the near loss of another.

# CHAPTER 13

# CLINT EASTWOOD MAKES MY DAY

For a while after my kids flew the coop to out-of-state schools, I behaved like Pippi Longstocking. In 1992, when thirteen-year-old Seamus left home for boarding school in Colorado, I found a way to make the most of his sudden absence. I ate popcorn and ice cream for dinner, and canceled client appointments on the spur of the moment to go to the movies in the middle of the afternoon. After standing in line at Santa Monica Seafood to buy a pathetic single piece of fish, something I had previously pitied in others, I would abandon that dinner option once I got home and think, *I don't want fish; I want chocolate chip cookies.* And I would bake cookies instead.

Like a younger sibling moving into the newly vacated room of a college-bound older sibling, I persuaded Seamus's piano teacher, Herb Donaldson, to allow me to move into Seamus's Thursday afternoon lesson time. I had studied all through college but had not played in years. The great Mr. Donaldson gradually coaxed my long-abandoned skills out. I found great solace in playing, and made my weekly lesson a scheduling priority.

My empty nest had filled up with new clients and bigger— and riskier—cases. Without the kids, I threw myself into them, eliminating the void. I was moving into the height of my career. In fact, I was so busy that I sent letters on Post-its to my children's various campuses. When they saw Bronwyn reading the yellow stickies, her roommates would comment, "Oh, another letter from your mom?"

On Bronwyn's twenty-first birthday, I was in trial when I realized I hadn't gotten her anything for her birthday. Desperate not to blow it entirely, I sent her the only thing I could with a phone call—a gift basket of fruit. She hasn't let me forget that one. We laugh about it now, but back then, not so much.

One day in 1993, I received a phone call from a powerhouse lawyer with whom I was in litigation on a cutting-edge and high-profile sex discrimination case dubbed "The Board vs. The Babe" by *Time* magazine. I represented the female plaintiff CFO—who, I contended, should have been promoted to CEO under the corporation's succession plan. My colleague's client was a key witness and the outgoing corporate CEO. We two lawyers had hit it off as litigators in combat sometimes do, especially when our clients' interests are in alignment against the other side. We took turns tormenting our opposing counsel, who seemed to have no sense of humor. In my experience, good trial lawyers engage in edgy humor as part of the game, and the other lawyer and I played it up.

The potential case he was calling about involved celebrities and a major studio. But he was calling from his car, and he said he'd call me back with the names of the potential parties later over a landline if I was interested in the case. (We were just becoming aware around that time of rampant eavesdropping on cell phone calls.) When I asked if he thought there was a case, he said he did, but most people in town wouldn't want to take on the studio.

Unlike attorneys in the entertainment business, I had little to lose. I was a lone plaintiff's lawyer who represented women and other employees in sex, age, and race discrimination cases against big corporate employers. The David vs. Goliath scenario was still my specialty.

I had been hoping for a case involving the entertainment industry, where I knew women were treated worse than in many other industries. But everyone knew that to bring a case was to kiss a career good-bye, so the outrages went on, unchallenged. My jaw had dropped when I'd once heard a prominent entertainment attorney dismiss the web of conflicts of interest in the entertainment business by saying, "Conflicts are contacts."

I told my caller I was in.

That's how I met diminutive Sondra Locke, who had just completed a sketchy development contract at Warner Brothers—one created as part of her settlement of "palimony" claims against her long-time love, Clint Eastwood, Warner Brothers' biggest star.

Sondra, a waiflike actress with a perfect, creamy complexion, arrived in a classic yellow Mercedes coupe. Dressed casually in vintage beige slacks, a long-sleeved blouse, and a vest for our first meeting, she was clearly no spendthrift. My Victorian house-turned-office building appealed to her tastes, and it became an inviting and comforting environment for her as it had for other women I represented.

She brought along her contracts, which appeared to be recycled from other Warner Brothers deals. In the negotiations and the drafting of the documents, an expensive Beverly Hills lawyer had represented her. I was shocked to think lawyers were being paid huge fees to recycle these embarrassingly bad contracts from other deals, with the previous names blacked out and new names interlineated. I also couldn't imagine why a lawyer representing her would have agreed to submit her palimony lawsuit against a powerful man to the secrecy and mischief of binding arbitration, and away from the publicly transparent open courtroom, but hers had done so. The results were not favorable to her.

She professed to have been blindsided by her recent discovery that Warner Brothers had never intended to make a movie with her. Sondra had learned from an insider on the Warner Brothers lot that her deal with Warner Brothers was a ruse, made solely to accommodate Clint as part of a scheme to put an end to her pending palimony case against him. After researching the meaning of "pay or play" in industry contracts, I dubbed it the "We screw everybody because we can" clause. The well-established law of contracts, the covenant of good faith and fair dealing, the industry insisted, did not apply to them.

Thus was born Locke v. Warner Bros., a case that would make new law on "pay or play" contracts in the California Court of Appeal, but only after being tossed out with a flourish by a cranky Burbank judge who called me "little lady." As Judge Murphy announced dismissal of our case, he said, "Take it up, and May God have mercy on your soul."

Judge Murphy had just handed Clint Eastwood to us on a platter. Before entering judgment dismissing the case, he had denied my motion to bring Clint into the Warner Brothers case as a defendant. Instead of protecting the studio and its biggest star, Judge Murphy had unwittingly moved the studio shield out of the way, giving me a pretty good shot at the iconic cowboy.

Clint had made admissions in a deposition in Locke v. Warner Brothers that supported a separate lawsuit against him.

So I filed a case against Clint Eastwood—Locke v. Eastwood—which went to jury trial.

In September 1996, I found myself standing and arguing before a judge, a jury, and a packed gallery in the little courtroom of the old Western-style Burbank courthouse, nestled in the foothills of the San Gabriel Mountains. I was dressed demurely in heels and a skirt suit with a crisp white collar and cuffs. Like my Catholic school uniforms of long ago, my sartorial choices as a lawyer did more to conceal than reveal who I was—or at least what I had planned.

We alleged, and I now had to prove, that Clint had tricked Sondra into dropping her claims to many millions in her palimony case against him, in exchange for a bogus movie development deal with his studio, Warner Brothers.

Several years earlier, well-placed mutual friends of hers and Clint's, Al Ruddy and Lili Zanuck, had approached Sondra when she was recovering from a double mastectomy to tell her what Clint was proposing. In a nutshell, she was advised that she could either take the deal with Clint and work, or spend the rest of her life in court like Michele Marvin, whose years-long case against star Lee Marvin yielded only grief. Sondra wanted to direct. She dropped her pending case against Clint and signed a three-year $1.5 million pay-or-play development deal with Warner Brothers. And then she was ignored.

As I stood there on that September day, I held in my hand what I considered the smoking gun: printed cost runs from Clint's movie *Unforgiven*, showing Sondra's deal as a cost of that movie, on which she had done no work. The money paid to Sondra was, I argued, "laundered" by Warner Brothers to conceal that it was really from Clint, and that her deal was in reality designed to be a career dead-end.

I was asking a judge to allow me to publicly string up the

hometown boy with evidence of shady financial doings that are routine legerdemain in the movie industry. I felt like the Clint Eastwood character in *Unforgiven*, come to town to avenge the woman whose face was slashed: "But Your Honor, the cost sheets showing payment of Ms. Locke's $1.5 million contract from *Unforgiven* prove the fraud at the heart of this entire case. They are the device of the fraud. Ms. Locke never worked on *Unforgiven*. Mr. Eastwood's company Malpaso produced it, and yet they show her being paid from the production costs of that movie . . . with laundered funds. I have to put them into evidence to prove my case. It shows he hoodwinked her into a deal that was a dead-end for her career."

Judge David Schacter rolled his eyes with impatience and scoffed at my focus on the California Evidence Code. He shut me down, citing no legal authority for refusing to admit evidence that was clearly admissible. "Ms. Garrity, you can just put Mr. Eastwood on the stand and ask him the questions. Let him tell his story. You don't need the documents unless he denies it and you need impeachment. This case is not about documents."

The unsympathetic and media-savvy Burbank judge was having his fun as King of the Mountain; he had just dared and double-dared me to engage in a shootout with Eastwood in his studio's hometown.

I continued to argue: "But I shouldn't have to put him on the stand." I almost convinced myself that I didn't want to cross-examine Clint Eastwood.

Judge Schacter loved being in show business. Just before 11:30 A.M., he bellowed his order with a noisy flourish of his gavel: "We will be in recess for fifteen minutes and you, Ms. Garrity, will call your next witness or rest your case when we return."

There were fifteen minutes remaining before the noon break on this Friday morning, and we were not scheduled to come back that afternoon. The potential for last-minute drama is always there before adjournment, and I intended to use it to its maximum effect.

I could hear Eastwood's gaggle of lawyers, from several of Los Angeles's major entertainment and litigation firms, chortling and high-fiving on the other side of the courtroom. The tall cowboy and his posse were convinced that this case would be tossed out, just like the one against Warner Brothers had been. They believed my smoking gun had been tossed on the heap, and my whole case along with it.

I probably deserved some neener-neener after what I had done to them earlier in the week. After days of being nagged to tell them when I planned to call Clint to the stand, I'd told his team it would likely be Wednesday morning, so he had arrived fully made up, dressed in a blue in-the-line-of-fire suit, and armed with filmography boards depicting his many films over the years. The Academy Award–winning director and actor had been visibly angry at his lawyers when I hadn't called him to the stand, blaming them, not me. Now he believed he was in the clear. But I was gunning for Clint, and planned to take him in an ambush. Fortunately, I still had a bullet or two in my chamber.

Judge Schacter had made it clear that he wanted to see Clint on the stand, to see some live action. And there was someone else who wanted to see me wrangle with Clint: Seamus, who had taken to tormenting me by calling our Australian shepherd, Ziggy, to the whistled tune from *The Good, the Bad and the Ugly*. He was studying film at Santa Monica College and knew all there was to know about so-called spaghetti Westerns, and he held in high regard the hombre at the defense table. He was in the gallery that day, and when he heard Schacter repeatedly holler, "Ms. Garrity, the jury instructions are going to kill you," he figured the judge was just enjoying the game, and that he liked me because he was smiling. Some judges do enjoy tormenting lawyers, so I thought perhaps he was right.

There was a noir-type dynamic peculiar to Los Angeles in play here: the big male celebrity brought low by a blonde. Eastwood was counting on being the sympathetic party—the big star being knocked over (as he put it to reporters) by a gold-digging woman. At day's end, he started leaving through the front door of the courthouse, escorted by star-struck sheriff's deputies, into the waiting scrum of press, instead of sneaking out the back door as he had in the beginning of trial.

While Clint treated Sondra as if she were a mere nuisance, his disdain for me was developing its own personality. In her memoir, *The Good, the Bad, and the Very Ugly*, Sondra said he looked at me "with hatred." One day he fed the press hordes by trashing my handling of the case as "some kind of dime novel." He added, "No good deed goes unpunished."

Every morning, I hauled my boxes of documents—piled three-high onto a folding trolley—with my left hand and a stuffed boxlike litigation bag in my right as I walked from the parking lot behind the courthouse around the corner, down the sidewalk past the press, and up the steps to court by myself. I was no sylph-like Ally McBeal in the rear-view shots carried on the nightly news, though I did sport the fashionable above-the-knee skirts and heels of the mid-nineties. My horrified sister Maura, in a late-night phone call from Wisconsin, advised me to "lose the drag bag." I was hefting boxes like a longshoreman. How I longed for the seventies, when, for a short time, we wore pantsuits and flats to court.

My opposition, a founding partner of a big firm, had lots of hired hands to do this work, and he always arrived elegantly clad and without breaking a sweat despite the 100-degree heat.

I repeated my beast-of-burden act returning to my car at

the end of the day. One afternoon my sacred cargo tipped over and fell all over the intersection in back of the courthouse, in front of a dark green GMC Yukon. I only looked his way long enough to realize that it was Clint behind the wheel. I had intended to apologize to the stalled driver. Now I didn't know what to do except rush about gathering up the paper that was halting traffic and hoping he didn't hit the gas. *Shit, shit, shit,* I thought as I scrambled. It called for a double martini at the daily after-court roundup Sondra and I had at a nearby pub.

At eleven forty-five that Friday morning, I stood and addressed Judge Schacter, turning ever so slightly toward opposing counsel's table as I did.

"The plaintiff calls Clint Eastwood."

There was scrambling and shuffling of paper at the defense table. Clint, not used to having anyone else call the shots, finally sauntered to the witness stand and, glaring at me, took a seat. He was an actor without his script on a day he had not expected to be called. He was pissed and did nothing to hide it. He had good reason to fear that if he responded incorrectly, all the financial shenanigans kept hidden so far might well be admitted into evidence. As the press came crashing through the door after the break, fresh from calling in the most recent ruling in his favor, Clint gave me every admission I needed to prove my case against him.

Yes, he sent his pal Al Ruddy to offer Sondra a deal at Warner Brothers in exchange for her dropping her palimony case against him.

Yes, the $1.5 million paid to her under the deal came from him.

No, she had not worked on *Unforgiven.*

Yes, he had made the deal secretly with WB President Terry Semel and agreed to indemnify Warner Brothers if there was any cost to them.

Yes, he had paid it off early, by the beginning of the second year of the three-year deal.

No, Sondra had not been told about it.

Yes, she would likely have considered it important in making the deal.

I was leading him, and he was going right along with me, so I moved in for the kill: "You knew at the time you sent Al Ruddy to talk to her that she was recovering from a double mastectomy and chemotherapy, true?"

"I thought it was one."

Several of the jurors gasped.

Perhaps he was thinking, theatrically, of the Amazon women who, as legend has it, cut off one breast to make spear throwing easier before going into battle. I waited him out. My aim was true. As Clint's character Blondie advised in *The Good, the Bad and the Ugly*, "When you have to shoot, shoot, don't talk."

I had aimed. And fired. And stopped talking.

There was no question the morning and the week belonged to us. But the game was far from over. On Monday the defense would start their case, and I had no illusions that we weren't in for some serious blows. Among them was the little problem of Sondra's long marriage to Gordon, an openly gay man with whom she had bonded for life as a child in Tennessee. Gordon lived in a medieval-looking Hollywood house Clint had bought for Sondra, and had been a frequent visitor to the Carmel ranch when Clint and Sondra were there.

The Hollywood house was a virtual set shrouded in tall hedges and trees, the walls and furniture all dark woods, with pointy rooftops peeking over the hedgerows, leaded windowpanes, arched doorways, and stone floors. Like the Storybook Land ride at Disneyland, fairy tale buffs Sondra and Gordon had fashioned a fantasy world beyond the portals. Oddly, the interior immediately brought to mind "The Bishop's Bedroom," a hidden and ornate paneled chamber at St. Mary's Academy, my high school. One evening the preceding December when I arrived for a holiday champagne, I was left outside in the rain as inside I could hear a furious scurrying amid hushed voices. Shivering in the dark, I felt like a character from Thomas Hardy or Dickens. Suddenly the door ceremoniously opened, and there stood Gordon, backlit by candlelight in a floor-length dressing gown, red-striped socks, curly elf shoes, and a bed cap. Beside him stood his boyfriend, who held aloft a silver tray with bubbling champagne flutes. Sondra stage-managed the festivities; this was just the opening scene. The hours of work that had to have gone into this display was astonishing.

Each room was suitable for an FAO Schwartz Christmas window. Perfectly placed twinkling tree lights illuminated each vignette, and under and around each tree were amazing antique toys, trains, wagons, trucks, cars, and dolls. Sondra and Gordon called each other "Hobbit."

Back in court, it was difficult to imagine that a Los Angeles judge and jury were going to find against a huge star like Clint and in favor of my client, especially when she'd remained married (albeit to a gay man) throughout their relationship. The defense case promised to be scandalous.

When Judge Schacter let the jury go for the weekend, I wondered if that was the last I would see of them. He indicated we would be *in camera* and not need a jury for the afternoon. And he hadn't yet ruled on several motions he had been taking under submission during trial. I wondered if he had already decided to grant the defense motions and toss out our case.

After several hours of arguing by the lawyers, Judge Schacter announced, "The motion for nonsuit is under submission. Mr. Fisher, be ready with your witnesses on Monday."

A motion for nonsuit is a routine motion made by the defense at the end of the plaintiff's presentation of evidence, asking the court to dismiss the case before the defense even puts on any evidence. It is usually denied. Taking the motion under submission was the next best thing, because it meant we still had a shot at a verdict.

Yippee! The last thing our jury had heard before the weekend were the admissions of our movie-star hero . . . who had indeed made my day. It would be another two-martini roundup, and I needed it. I was starting to think I might just get to argue to the jury after all, and win or lose, that would be a victory.

By Monday morning I was jumping out of my skin, wishing I hadn't gotten pregnant and missed medical school and the convent, wishing I could have been a proper wife and mother who stayed at home. During a trial, I was focused on slaying the dragons, but in the off hours I was nuts. Sleeping only three or four hours a night, and not necessarily consecutive hours, was my standard. Even early-morning meditation and laps in the pool sometimes weren't enough. To restore my trial swagger I needed a sexual romp. By the time I got back to court, I had to be firing on all cylinders. So Monday before dawn I phoned Hank, who knew my trial protocols. We were not a couple just then, and he was seeing other women. (We had gone through several breakups, all attributable to my quixotic decisions, and when I once said we had been together fifteen years, he responded that it was "a net of twelve.")

Me: "Hi. I'm in jury trial today. Is anyone else there?"

Him: "No." *Yawn.* "Come on over."

For me, there is something inherently sexual about trial— the give and take, the sparring and foreplay, the power shifts, the cat-and-mouse tussle, and of course, the climax and release of each day. I needed to release that energy outside the court.

Men, it seems to me, approach this differently, and they channel all their sexual energy into the fight when they are in trial, like athletes saving it all up for the game.

With the army arrayed against me Monday morning, it was a fair bet they had come up with something over the two-day break with which to blindside me. By this point in my career I knew the other side spent an inordinate amount of time profiling me. But on my side of the case there was only me and limited resources. Like a boxer, I stayed in constant motion, trying to be prepared for anything in trial—and consequently, some of my greatest moments were sort of surprising, even to me.

But, alas, there were no great surprises. Clint's team had not expected our case to even get to trial, and most certainly, not this quickly. Worse, in cross-examination Clint had showed anger at me in front of a jury—a mistake. The big tough cowboy surrounded by his Beverly Hills gunslingers had made himself out to be the victim of the waiflike girl sitting at the plaintiff's table. It called to mind the Catholic Church hierarchy, all male, who cast women as the occasion of evil, even burning a few at the stake for daring to challenge the authority of men in dresses and funny hats. On the other hand, we have now all seen powerful male celebrities try to evade accountability in front of juries, even to the point of getting away with murder. Lawyers for O.J. Simpson, Robert Blake, and Phil Spector (who was finally convicted in a retrial), to name a few, were all somehow able to cast the killers as victims of the slaughtered women in their lives.

At the last moment, Clint's attorney, Ray Fisher, called Sondra back to the stand.

As she stood up to go, Sondra whispered to me, "They're about to see just why I was nominated for an Academy Award."

Ray opened with a leading question: "You testified this

morning that you caught Stephen Beale going through your purse and that is why you fired him, correct?"

"Yes."

Mr. Fisher showed her a transcript of her deposition and led again: "You didn't tell me that when I asked you for all the reasons you fired him, did you, even though you were allowed as much time as you wanted to give any and all reasons?"

"No." She remained calm and poised.

"You didn't call Warner Brothers' security when you observed this, did you?"

"No." She was unflustered, and even appeared to be enjoying this.

"Why didn't you call security or mention that purse incident in your deposition?"

Sondra leaned into the microphone and softly said, "His brother was dying of AIDS, and I didn't want to make it more difficult for him to get another job."

What Ray couldn't have known and therefore could not have asked was the question I was now asking myself: *Why did this woman who takes notes about everything never mention this extreme act of dishonesty to me, her lawyer?* Ray was suggesting that Sondra's testimony was suspect because she had not divulged it when she should have in her deposition. I was troubled because I, her lawyer for the last several years, was hearing this particular tale for the first time right here in trial. If it had happened, I reasoned, she should have told me long ago.

I swept aside my misgivings and dove into my closing, insisting that the evidence proved Clint had colluded with Warner Brothers to snooker Sondra into dropping her palimony suit in exchange for a development deal that was actually designed to be a dead-end to her career. The jurors were attentive. But who knows what a jury will do?

Just after they went to the jury room to start deliberations, Ray and I were standing at the clerk's desk waiting for some final changes in the written instructions. Clint loped up alongside me. There I was, all five foot three of me, sandwiched between these six-foot-four pillars of power, and they let me know just how inconsequential I was.

"This will be the fastest verdict in history," Ray crowed.

The two of them moved closer, as if I were truly not there, and Clint's right hand came up against my left and stayed there. It was as cold as ice. The tall boys exchanged glances and laughed knowingly.

Waiting for a jury verdict is like waiting for your water to break in the last days of pregnancy. You want to get it over with, but you don't want to go through it. You wonder why on earth you ever thought this whole project was a good idea. You bargain with God to get you out of this with a good result and to give you the strength to handle a bad result. You jump every time the jury has a question, because when the court calls you in, you think this could be it.

Then you turn into a psychic, trying to read the tea leaves to figure out what the question really means—which way the panel is leaning. You try to read their faces when they file in. They, on the other hand, try hard to not let it appear that they have any leanings at all.

This jury had several questions before they adjourned for the weekend. We wouldn't get a decision until the following week.

On Saturday morning, I got a call from Ray. I was sitting cross-legged on the floor after my morning meditation practice, so I was blessedly relaxed and calm. This time of the day, in the tiny space in my room, away from the din of the rest of the household, before a little altar with sacred objects from the various parts of my life, restored me. Sometimes, I would sit with eyes closed and visualize the faces of the jury panel where they sat in the courtroom, praying for a just result, a win. Could this call be an answer?

"Peggy, can we talk about settling this case before the jury comes back and ruins your life or mine?"

As I mentally put my gun and holster back on, I responded, "But Ray, they can't ruin my life. I live on the edge."

We talked a bit, he made an offer, and we continued that way over the next two days. I was relaying the offers and counter-offers to Sondra, and he was going back and forth with Clint, who was reportedly at his Carmel ranch with no plans to return to court. We finally reached agreement. Clint's lawyers proposed calling the court to tell the judge we had reached a settlement and have the judge let the jury go, but I refused. I wanted a court record.

When we arrived Monday morning, Ray sportingly tried again to get rid of the jury before we had a deal set into the record. He had settlement documents typed up for us to sign—pages and pages of them. There was no reason to sign these and lots of reasons not to. By now I was suspicious of everything the other side proposed. No more deals that could be breached or disavowed.

Without even reading them, I declined and said we would just go ahead and let the jury continue to deliberate, as if our discussions had never taken place. Without a court record sealing the deal, there was no enforceable settlement agreement, and letting the jury go would be tantamount to dismissing the case. Finally, we went into the judge's chambers with the court reporter and recited the agreement. It would be binding and enforceable by the court, the same as a judgment. The amount would also be confidential, so long as it was paid by the end of the week and we didn't have to bring an enforcement action.

*     *     *

Our team celebrated with a champagne brunch at the elegant Hotel Bel-Air, one of my favorite spots in Los Angeles—an illusion of the French countryside, ponds filled with white swans and all, nestled among oak trees, just minutes away from the bustle of Sunset Boulevard and the 405 Freeway. Upon returning to my office, we were confronted with press from all over the world; media trucks with towers were parked in front of my little blue Craftsman house-turned-office. The picket-fence-enclosed rose garden, in full bloom from the September Santa Ana heat, provided a lovely backdrop for the pictures taken during the interviews, and Sondra looked truly happy and victorious, posing with a huge yellow rose plucked from my garden.

Colin, who by now had several years of experience at CAA, a talent agency and Hollywood powerhouse, quickly arranged for a podium to be placed on the steps where I could take questions from the press. He had also already contacted the courtroom television artist, Mona Shafer Edwards, to purchase the drawings that had been shown on the nightly news. He had gotten to her minutes ahead of Ray's office, so we got our pick; the drawings now grace the walls in my home office.

The next day, a whole new game started. Ray messengered over a letter that asserted, "We saw you and your client on the news last night and are of the opinion that you are in violation of the confidentiality provision of the settlement agreement. Consequently, we are not bound by the agreement for payment. When a reporter asked if the settlement was for $7 million, Sondra nodded her head in agreement."

That hadn't happened, and that wasn't the settlement. I messengered back a response that in no uncertain terms let him know what I would do to protect my client. "It appears the settlement was just a ruse to derail a jury that was going against you and for us. This is starting to look like Eastwood's M.O., fraudulently inducing a settlement agreement to get rid of pending lawsuits against him. If payment is not made as agreed by Friday, I will file another fraud case on Monday, and this one will name you and your firm as a party."

After a bit more jockeying, we met at the courthouse. It was over. Sondra and I had our money and our victory.

# CHAPTER 14

# STRIKE THREE

In 1997, the year I turned fifty, my whole world turned upside down . . . again.

Just before Christmas 1984, the kids and I had moved to the port in the storm they would call home for the next sixteen years, and one they still rhapsodize about as perfect. Our Spanish-style house on 25th Street in Santa Monica, just north of Montana Avenue, was small—an incomplete remodel I bought from a contractor who desperately needed to sell it and agreed to carry the financing for ten years, making my purchase possible at a time when I was dealing with residual credit issues from my second divorce. The seller even asked me to move in before the close of escrow and laughed off my unsolicited legal advice not to let the buyer take possession before the close of escrow. We established a rapport, and when I discovered construction shortcuts, like lack of permits, etc., we were able to negotiate a resolution that suited us both.

The house had beautiful Spanish tile floors, and four bedrooms if I included the illegally converted garage. I could see that part of the house as a bedroom and man cave for my two boys. To the kids' delight, the house also had a small front yard and a dog run on the side, as well as a pool. (I later learned, to my chagrin, that Seamus and his chums routinely jumped off the roof into that pool.) We were close to schools, parks, a movie theater, restaurants and shops, and Yoga Works. Seamus, until then a captive of the canyons, was delirious that he had sidewalks to travel, and quickly introduced himself around and made it his business to get to know everyone in the neighborhood—what they did, what cars they drove, even what flowers they were planting. On our first day there, he announced that he was never moving again.

Now, thirteen years later—just when I seemed to be hitting my stride as a trial lawyer, getting great cases and great results, being recognized in legal publications, and speaking by invitation at law schools and trial lawyer conventions—I was being leveled by illness for the first time. In January, I felt a small, painful rash on my right side. Soon it spread and turned my whole right torso into a sheet of fire, and I consulted a doctor for the first time in ages. He phoned me a few days later with terrifying news.

"Your blood tests are back and you are really sick. You have no T-cells. You need to come in right away."

Having litigated AIDS-discrimination cases, I knew what that meant. I gazed out at the ocean as my world slipped into slow motion, thinking, *This can't be how it ends for me, can it? This is impossible. I haven't had a life yet. I have four kids.*

"You're not telling me I have AIDS, are you?" I asked. "What were the results of that test?"

He rustled some papers as he responded, "Oh, did we do that test? Let me look . . . It's negative. But I have had several patients who had false negatives. It doesn't mean anything."

As instructed, I made an appointment to see him that afternoon. But before going, after considering this absurdity, my terror turned to anger at his callousness. I came to my senses, sort of. I canceled that appointment and made an appointment for that afternoon with another doctor.

The pronouncement of the second doctor both relieved and alarmed me. "You do not have AIDS," he said, "but you are sick." He told me that my adrenal glands were depleted and my immune system shot. I would need lots of rest to fully recover, he said. As he put it, "you need to change your life." He also told me I was lucky my wake-up call wasn't cancer. I had shingles. The pain was deep into the nerves, and the next three months were agonizing, so much so that I was unable to work. I was depleted emotionally, physically, and spiritually.

I spent most of January, February, and March 1997 out at the Malibu beach house that I bought with Hank the year before, shortly after we had gotten back together. Now I was like a wounded animal, pushing him away, wanting to be left alone. I think he was in denial that I was ill and powerless, because he had never seen me that way. "You're a warrior," he often said. Not now. I was too depleted to even get mad. I wanted him, impossibly, to just know what I wanted and needed, and then take care of me. I realized that at the core of it all was my mother's refusal to accept weakness of any kind in me, including illness. Like I once had as a child, I crept away to get well on my own.

I spent the days watching the whales from my rocking chair, wrapped in a blanket, when I was in too much pain to lie down. For hours I stared out at the sea. The annual migration of the gray whales was awe-inspiring, but the enormous blue whales I spotted several times impressed me even more. These behemoths leaped into the air, defying their size as well as the increasing contamination of our oceans, showing me what survival looked like. They seemed to be egging me on to beat my illness.

Downsizing my life was essential, I realized, especially now that my kids were grown. So I set out to let go of everything I could survive without, relieving all the economic pressure I could, especially the huge mortgage on the Santa Monica house. I had refinanced it many times over the years to pay for the kids' tuition and room and board, paying no attention to the interest rate on the loans as long as I could get the money out. Sometimes I felt like I was running in front of a train. I was in serious debt, and exhausted beyond anything I had ever known.

In spring 1997, just after turning fifty, I broke off my relationship with Hank for the last time. Maybe if we had met earlier I would have been able to have a relationship with that kind, loving, and tolerant man, but I finally realized I didn't want to be married and face another potential disaster. All my energy reserves were depleted. I sold my Santa Monica house and used the proceeds to pay off my debt and buy Hank out of the beach house. I remodeled it into a little cottage, and moved out to Malibu.

With that move, my monthly housing expense dropped to $2,500, and I paid off most of my debt. I felt drawn to the beach in Malibu as if it were Lourdes. Daily walks on the beach and the rhythm of the tides, the night skies, and the nature at the beach restored my health.

But I wasn't ready to give up my crazy life as a trial lawyer, and I had some juicy cases awaiting my attention, including Strohmeyer v. Western Digital, a sex discrimination in employment case, and the Locke v. Warner Brothers appeal, which had yet to be argued and decided. Life was going to go on, newly fraught with developments I could not have imagined. I was out of one wood, but I suddenly found myself in a jungle.

# CHAPTER 15

# TURNING POINTS

Still fatigued, I wondered how I was going to make it through all that I had committed to professionally. Horseback rides through the mountains in Malibu gave me surprising strength, however—especially in the spring, when wildflowers covered the hillsides. Chocolate lilies, Indian paintbrush, blue lupine, poppies, and so many others would pop up all along the riding trails. At some points, tall wild mustard blanketed the hills and enveloped me in yellow. I was using equine therapy before I knew it had a name.

The healing power of horses has drawn me to them since I was a little girl in Wisconsin and galloped all over the countryside with my friend Bunny, who lived on a ranch on the outskirts of town. After her mother died from a fall down the stairs when we were in second grade, Bunny and I became inseparable. Over the years we spent long hours on horseback; it was the only place she seemed happy, especially when the horses ran full speed. Now, in my weakened, and awakened, condition, horseback riding through the mountain trails of Malibu beckoned me.

One Saturday morning, about a year after the Locke v. Eastwood trial, I was out for a ride on mountainside trails through Bonsall Canyon in Malibu with a freelance writer named Deanne. We had become friends and riding companions, renting horses from the same ranch almost every Saturday.

As we mounted our trusty middle-aged quarter horses and headed out to the trail, Deanne came up alongside me with some news: her agent had sent her a script to rewrite for Sondra Locke.

"It looks a lot like your IBM case," she told me, explaining that Sondra had a deal for a series with a cable channel. The show was to follow the lawyer handling the case. And, said Deane, "It sounds like you."

As Deanne filled me in, I realized the story was indeed my trial of the IBM case. I recalled how Sondra had attended virtually every day of the IBM trial, and how she'd chummed up to many of my clients, as well as my kids, at my frequent backyard barbecues. How long, I wondered, had she been writing and marketing the script? What else was in it? The blurring of boundaries between my personal and professional lives—occasioned by my need to wear many hats at once, as well as just plain bad judgment—had allowed this betrayal to happen. It wasn't the first, nor would it be the last, time someone tied to Hollywood pedaled my cases as their own original script material.

Perhaps it was my small-town upbringing and being the daughter of a funeral director. There were no boundaries. My dad's professional services were so much more than professional that the townspeople saw him as family. When he died, people in the tiny town of 5,000 lined up around the block of our funeral home to pay respects, and everyone I spoke with had a deeply personal story of their interaction with Dad. Some spoke of his secret deliveries of food to their families when they were in need, others of his helping their kids get scholarship help at the Catholic high schools.

As Deanne and I started into an easy trot, I told her that Sondra's producer had presented me with an agreement at one point that would allow them to use me as a character in a show about sexual harassment, and I'd declined. I hadn't taken the producer seriously when he'd said, "The question is whether you will sue."

Resorting to my smart-ass ways I quipped to Deanne. "She probably has my character sleeping with all the bailiffs, right?"

She just laughed.

*   *   *

The Monday following my conversation with Deanne, I wrote the cable executives handling the show and informed them I had not given, and would not give, my consent to be portrayed in any script. I would sue them. Shortly after this call, an entertainment lawyer phoned who said he was representing Sondra.

"You can't interfere with this project," he said, "because you are Sondra's lawyer and you have a conflict."

His position appeared to be that by virtue of my undertaking Sondra's legal representation, my life had become property that she could sell as her own. This was nonsense.

Following this exchange, Sondra wrote me a letter informing me that I had "interfered with something [she] very much needed and wanted." I was still her attorney of record on the appeal of the Warner Brothers summary judgment, however. So I worked on.

Months later, after oral argument, the court of appeal reversed the summary judgment granted by Judge Murphy and remanded Sondra's case for trial in a widely publicized, precedent-setting decision that created a roadmap for retrial. Warner Brothers' broad interpretation of "pay or play" would no longer be the rule in such contracts.

With this ruling, the stage was set for an enormous award of punitive damages; they would be based on the net worth of the defendant, which was a daunting number for Warner Brothers. A case that had been regarded as a loser four years earlier when I filed it, and more so when the trial court tossed it out on summary judgment, was being born again as a blockbuster worth many millions.

Although I was still not fully recovered, and was cognizant of the growing distance between me and Sondra, I dove into preparation for the Warner Brothers trial on remand, frequently falling asleep with transcripts and exhibits strewn all over my bed. While I was doing this, Sondra started shopping for a new lawyer. With the road map created by the appellate decision, she had no trouble finding one. Under the circumstances, I decided it was unwise to expend any more of myself to keep the case.

This second settlement, I learned from a reporter—made possible only as a result of the case law made because I pursued the appeal, without pay—was for many millions more than the settlement with Clint had been. Payment for my services for what I had done in the Warner Brothers case through the trial court and the appeal would come out of the settlement, I was sure. This was standard.

I was wrong.

I had to sue Sondra to get paid, although my payment would not have cost her a dime more than what was already going to legal fees, since it would simply have come out of her attorney's one-third contingency fee.

The near destruction of my health and the realization that

my idealism might have blinded me to reality were life-changing events. I had always seen my clients, mostly women, as righteous, and their fights as life-or-death struggles into which I'd leaped with abandon. In short, I'd spent most of my adult life in fight-or-flight mode. My law practice was more of a crusade than a law practice. I'd become one with their cases—totally identified with their cause. Everything had been black and white. Now I was forced to see that my clients might not always have been completely truthful, that I might have won when, if trials are a search for truth, I should have lost. I might have represented as facts to the court things that weren't factual.

It had taken a debilitating illness for me to see all this, but once I did, I never looked at cases the same way again. And it was never again as much fun. However, my law practice was maturing. In the coming years, it would go in new directions and become meaningful in new ways.

## • CHAPTER 16 •

# TWO BIRDS WITH ONE STONE

In an eerie twist of fate, seven years after the trial for the Teak Dyer wrongful death case, I found myself representing another mother who'd lost her child to murder just before his high school graduation. This time, however, my client was the mother of the killer. When there is one murder, I suddenly realized, at least two mothers lose a child.

Early one morning, shortly after Memorial Day 1997, I was nestled in my sun-drenched cottage in Malibu, preparing jury instructions for an upcoming sex discrimination trial. I was relaxed and focused after a wonderful yoga and meditation practice in front of the fire, looking out over the ocean. This thirty-year-old trailer in the Point Dume Mobile Home Park had become my refuge. To make it my own and indulge my repressed feminine desires for pretty stuff, I had remodeled the "double-wide" with French doors, bamboo floors, and decks all around. I'd put a claw-foot tub in my tiny bathroom, hung a black antique wrought iron and crystal chandelier over the trestle dining table, and put matching sconces on the walls. To top it off, I'd placed a shiny new black baby grand piano in the middle of the room, where I could play as I looked out on the ocean. The solitude I so needed at this time in my life I found here.

I was suing Western Digital Corporation in Orange County on behalf of two women who had lost their jobs after many years—due, we were arguing, to the fact that the company had skewed a layoff to target women over fifty. Women represented 75 percent of the layoff; the company population, on the other hand, was 60 percent male.

One of my clients, Winnie Strohmeyer—a warm, smart, and funny woman—had been director of human resources for years when she was shoved aside by a much younger man she had trained. He once complained, "You remind me of my mother." This recent Stanford graduate was chummy with the boss and had nabbed Winnie's job in the so-called "layoff" while she was in Singapore on expatriate assignment. The CEO admitted to me in his deposition that after the layoff he walked into a human resources meeting and crowed, "Well, if it's not my all-white-male human resources boys."

We had beaten a summary judgment motion and were winning the important pre-trial motions. I was excited about getting our case in front of a jury—where, I was sure, the overwhelming statistical evidence that would come in through my renowned workplace expert, along with the cavalier admissions of the CEO, would make a big win for our side a near certainty.

Then a ringing phone shattered the peace in my ocean hideaway.

Mary, my tough-as-nails secretary, was sobbing. "Jeremy Strohmeyer killed the little girl in the casino. It's all over the television. The videotape shows him going into the bathroom after her. Oh, my God!"

I stared blankly at the ocean as I tried to process what she was saying. I knew she was referring to the murder of seven-year-old Sherrice Iverson in a casino in Prim, Nevada, which had horrified the country. I also knew the tape to which she referred because it had been played in a virtual continuous loop on the news since the grotesque strangulation slaying had been reported a week earlier. When I flipped on the television, there was the loop again, with the added footage of Jeremy, Winnie's son, being taken into custody.

I had spoken to Jeremy a few times when I had phoned his mother, and had no strong impression of him. But I couldn't fathom that he could have done this. He was an honor student at Long Beach High School, and set to graduate in two weeks.

I sounded in my own head like the neighbors interviewed by reporters on TV after one of their own has committed some unspeakable crime: "This is such a nice, quiet neighborhood. Things like that don't happen here. He was just a quiet, nice guy."

This was a repeat of the Teak story, but upside down and inside out. A graduation missed—but this time for the murderer. Murder and sexual assault—but this time the victim a little girl. The crime scene, a women's bathroom. In the sex-discrimination case I was preparing for trial, Dennis Gladwell, the same lawyer I had been in trial with seven years earlier in San Jose Federal Court when I learned Teak had been killed, was representing the corporate defendant. My stomach churned and I felt faint.

After I hung up, Winnie called me in tears and panic. Jeremy needed a lawyer. I knew her to be a devoted and deeply caring mother who had shepherded her brilliant, troubled, adopted son through increasingly turbulent times. Now she was seeing it all end in one of the most notorious child killings ever. *What is worse*, I thought, *being the mother of the murdered, or mother of the murderer?* Both are judged, even damned, by society. When a son murders a child, his mother is blamed. If a daughter is murdered after partying the night before graduation, her mother is adjudged negligent because she failed to prevent it. Though little Sherrice's father was the one who'd let her run around a Nevada casino the night she was killed, the media was asking, *Where was the mother?*

I was forced into an unpleasant self-examination. I recalled my utter lack of compassion for Garmanian's mother as the shy, well-dressed woman sat alone through the trial of her son.

Yet again, my good fortune contrasted sharply with my client's misfortune. Seamus, who had enjoyed school as a more or less extracurricular activity, had graduated from Crossroads High School, spent two years at Santa Monica college, and would now go off on a piano scholarship to Berklee College of Music in Boston. Winnie's son, Jeremy, had been a brilliant student who'd wanted to attend the Naval Academy, but he had fallen into a pit of darkness somewhere along the line—perhaps while the family was on assignment in Singapore—and now he would spend the rest of his life in prison. If he was lucky and didn't get the death penalty. Winnie, who had looked for a baby with special needs to adopt so long ago, never could have imagined what lay ahead. Knowing all this, I was, and still am, in awe of my blessings and sheer luck as the mother of my four.

I made a phone call to find out what I could for Winnie. Although the murder had happened out of state, Jeremy had been taken into custody at his home in the South Bay. I called Steve Kay, the head deputy of the Long Beach District Attorney's office and an expert on capital cases. He took my call right away. I knew Steve from my time as a clinical student in the Torrance branch of the Los Angeles District Attorney's office more than twenty years earlier. We had recently been put back in touch through a news reporter.

As soon as he picked up the phone, he said, "Your client needs a capital lawyer in Nevada. A good one. You should hear this kid's confession. He broke her neck." Kay had tried some of the grisliest and most notorious murder cases in Los Angeles, including Charles Manson's, yet this killing shocked him. Our call was brief, but he let me know just how bad the situation was.

I recommended that Winnie call Leslie Abramson, a brilliant and wily defense lawyer known for her motherly compassion for her clients—especially the Menendez brothers, who killed their parents, and in whose murder case she hung the first jury. Leslie was renowned for getting her clients past the death penalty, which Jeremy was certain to face. He needed her.

Seamus was grim-faced that evening as we talked at the kitchen table. He kept saying, "He's my age. He'll never go to the beach again. He can't ever just come home and kick it in the kitchen like this with his mom. It's so fucked. Did he really do it? He has to be crazy, right? His poor mom. She's so nice." Seamus had met her in my office on several occasions, and she had always joked around with him.

Seamus was right: She would never again sit at her kitchen table with her son.

At this stage in her civil case, there was no way to get out of going to trial without the agreement of the defendant, Western Digital, because, for strategic reasons, they had filed a cross-complaint. The CEO had taken the case as a personal attack, and he aimed to capitalize on my client's predicament with relish. They would not agree to a dismissal. Winnie and I would have to soldier on through trial, with the world wondering what on earth this mother was doing in a civil employment discrimination case while her son awaited trial on capital charges. She had no other choice.

Picking a jury under these circumstances was a nightmare. They would have to be asked in *voir dire* what impact the charges against Jeremy would have on their ability to be fair to his mother in this civil case. A few potential jurors were candid and said they couldn't be fair. The scary ones were those who said it didn't matter.

It got worse.

At the last minute, a new judge was assigned to the case. Notoriously hostile to sex-discrimination suits, his rulings were uniformly and unsurprisingly against us. Out of hand, and in clear error, he gutted our case by disallowing the statistical evidence at the heart of the case. He refused to allow our employment expert to testify, saying, "The jury doesn't need an expert on this case." The defense lawyer, Gladwell, was handed control of the courtroom, and he seemed to be enjoying his revenge for my multimillion-dollar verdict against him in the employment case we'd tried seven years earlier.

At one point, to show just how much control he had, Gladwell stood behind me and put his foot on the back of my chair, leaning over me as he questioned a witness. He also touched me repeatedly, on the shoulder or back or hand as he passed by, all in front of the jury. In sexual-discrimination cases, some defense lawyers pull this crap to show the jury that the complaining woman, and her lawyer, are making a big deal about nothing; trying to show that physical contact in the workplace is just friendly and normal. I didn't let him get away with it. After he had touched me several times, I awaited his next move, and when it came, I jumped from my chair and did my best to appear shocked. I needed the jury to see and feel my discomfort at his unwelcome touching—to counteract the message his constant "friendly" touching was intended to send.

When I objected discreetly at sidebar to defense counsel's

inappropriate behavior as textbook sexual harassment, reciting the whole thing into the record, the judge sneered at me. Then he retaliated by reprimanding me like a child in front of the jury for everything, from where I stood while questioning witnesses to my questions themselves, which he constantly interrupted. He wanted the jury to think I didn't know what I was doing.

I knew exactly what I was doing, however, and he knew it; and I knew what he was doing. He was trashing our case and me because he wanted to make sure we lost. This treatment of a lawyer on one side of the case is the biased judge's standard way of communicating to the jury his opinion of the case and which way they should go. He knew he couldn't just dismiss it without getting reversed on appeal, so he let me try it to verdict but butchered it to shreds.

I was making sure to recite everything into the record, including describing the physical contact and his refusal to do anything about it, so that a reviewing court would know what had occurred in this trial. Making a clear record was about all I could do for my client at this point. The judge got more and more furious with me, and I knew he was on the verge of citing me for contempt. I didn't care.

The defense verdict was no shock when it came back within an hour of the jury being sent out for deliberations. This was the only time in my entire career when I made a motion for a mistrial and right there on the spot made a barnburner of a speaking motion based upon the display of judicial bias. The red-faced judge denied the motion out of hand and vigorously denied he was biased. I knew all the while I wasn't going to take an appeal. My client didn't have the resources or the heart to continue on with this case; her son was facing the death penalty. But the judge didn't know that, so I pulled no punches as I made my record.

Winnie, who went to Mass every morning before court, was gracious and thoughtful in defeat, even as she faced her son's likely capital conviction. She sent me a card after the trial ended, which I still look to sometimes for perspective. On it was a drawing of a barn in the moonlight and the ancient verse: "Barn's burnt down . . . now I can see the moon."

# PART THREE

# CHAPTER 17

# DRAWN TO TROUBLE

One day in 2000, shortly before the Getty Museum's grand opening in a hillside fortress in Brentwood on the west side of Los Angeles, Nicholas Turner (formerly curator of drawings to the queen of England at the British Museum) and his art scholar wife came to see me. A local clergyman had referred them. We sat in my upstairs office. Dappled sunlight splashed down on them through the octagonal clerestory window near the pitch in the ceiling, casting them as characters in my vignette—and belying the unhappy purpose of this visit. Vintage William Morris silk screen wallpaper my decorators had insisted on importing from London as part of an authentic restoration over a decade earlier made the backdrop. I, the barrister, wore a skirt suit and high heels, as this meeting seemed to warrant a bit more than my casual office garb.

While I considered myself something of an expert in sexual harassment cases, this case would school me in a whole new world of legal intrigue: the efforts of a powerful art establishment to suppress scholarship that might expose it to ridicule, or worse.

As companies began to recognize sexual harassment as a workplace hazard in the 1990s, more than a few realized that it could also be wielded in their own interests, as sword or shield, to discredit an employee, whether true or not, whether abuser or victim.

Turner had been recruited away from the British Museum by the Getty to build its drawings collection several years earlier. Turner was now allegedly being stalked and harassed by a young woman subordinate with whom he had ended an affair. The Getty was aware of this, and was not only ignoring his complaints but was instructing Turner to give the young woman an excellent performance review because she "held all the cards."

Professorially dressed in a subdued plaid jacket with elbow patches at our first meeting, Turner pulled the veil back on the august façade of museums to reveal an industry rife with intrigue, duplicity, treachery, politically charged sexual liaisons and, perhaps even the murder of a master forger in Mexico. His brilliant and accomplished wife sat across from me as he confessed the sordid details of his ridiculous affair with his young staffer. In spite of the pain, I insisted that the spouses of my sexual harassment clients participate in some meetings, because their support was crucial both to the spouse and to the case. Otherwise the case was too hard to sell to a jury. In my experience, husbands often blame sexually abused wives. How much worse would it be to be married to and accepting of a man who cheated and then claimed harassment by the ex-lover?

Turner, who was also clearly in anguish, had refused the demands of his former paramour—so she began to prank call his wife, revealed to a competitor confidential bidding plans on a Raphael drawing, and corrupted important computer files. In my experience, the employer typically took the supervisor's side. Not here. The Getty defended the stalking female subordinate—because, I began to realize, its interests in discrediting Nicholas Turner coincided with hers. Here was an opportunity to exploit the law of sexual harassment to insulate the institution from an accusation it knew was coming: the presence of fakes in its storied collection.

Early on, Turner had identified a number of forgeries in the drawings collection at the Getty. His duties included authoring Volume IV of the official Getty *Drawings* catalog, where, as the drawings scholar, he discussed the six suspected forgeries in the Getty's touted Renaissance drawings collection. This didn't sit well with the "powers that be," especially as one of the forgeries hung in the hallway outside the office of the museum director, Deborah Gribbon. Worse, the forgeries upon which the Getty had expended millions appeared to have been acquired by Turner's predecessor—who had been having an affair with Gribbon. That predecessor, now ensconced at the New York Metropolitan, vigorously opposed the publication of the catalog, as it would cast doubt on his expertise and scholarship. I heard through the grapevine that he went as far as threatening the president of the Getty Trust that he would take action "to protect his interests."

It was widely known in the art world that the Getty had already spent $7 million to acquire a Greek Kouros sculpture that turned out to be a fake. The Getty was not the only institution to have been hoodwinked, of course. But Turner informed me that although forgeries exist in museums and collections throughout the world, they are not usually acknowledged because they constitute an embarrassment to the institution. He described the bustling black market fueled by the vast sums that institutions with huge endowments, such as the Getty, have and must expend every year. This was an environment ripe for manipulation. The Getty would do everything in their power to keep the identities of the other forgeries under wraps.

The forgeries Turner identified had an especially eye-popping provenance. They were likely the product of 20th-century master British forger Eric Hebborn, whose work Turner had studied. Hebborn had gone to great lengths to make his work appear authentic, including placing it on eighteenth-century archival paper and selecting artists to forge who often incorporated work from "the school"—as did, for example, Spanish artist Jusepe de Ribera.

I was captivated by the backstory, told by the rogue artist himself in his riveting autobiography, *Drawn to Trouble*. Turner gave me a copy as a gift, along with two of Hebborn's drawings, including a Hebborn self-portrait that Turner had acquired to study. I could tell by the way Turner smiled as he described Hebborn's tormented life that he admired this rascal and his wily schemes to sell phony art to phony people.

The troubled but talented Hebborn insisted he made forgeries not primarily to make money, though he enjoyed the fruits of his labor, but to expose the ignorance of an art world that had failed to recognize him. Someone took him seriously: shortly after publication of his confessional, he died outside his home in Mexico, his skull smashed in. But now, Hebborn might at last receive the recognition, and satisfaction, he sought, because the evidence in our case would show that scholars at the Getty and elsewhere had been bamboozled by his forgeries. This revelation was likely to be explosive in a case about sexual escapades in the August Getty Museum.

Turner's subordinate, he said, had first pleaded with him to continue the affair. "Everyone in the Getty has affairs," she cried. When Turner resisted, she threatened to "destroy" him. But Turner held his ground, rejecting her advances. True to her word, she next made a false and retaliatory accusation of sexual harassment against Turner.

The conduct of this subordinate fit the definition of quid pro quo sexual harassment. But the Getty dismissed the possibility of Turner having a legitimate complaint for sexual harassment (following common wisdom at the time), and instead of offering help, the museum had seized the opportunity to compromise Turner's professional and scholarly reputation. The Getty advised Turner that he had no claim, but his subordinate did. They instructed him to give the subordinate an excellent performance review rather than the unsatisfactory review he felt was appropriate.

As far as I was concerned, this was another example of a powerful institution using sexual harassment claims, and the possibility of such claims, to exercise control for its own purposes. I issued a letter laying out Turner's claims against his subordinate and demanded protection for him from the stalker. I wasn't surprised when the Getty rebuffed me. I immediately filed a case alleging sexual harassment—against both the museum and Turner's subordinate.

The lawsuit made headlines around the world. The *Los Angeles Times* called it "A Fly in the Getty's Punchbowl." European press likened it to the movie *Disclosure*. The news coverage was breathless but generally overlooked the issue of the forgeries—the issue I believed was at the heart of the case.

Since I was known for representing women in sexual harassment cases, friends of mine read the stories and called saying, "How could you represent that guy?" Even my kids took notice of the shift. Finally I had a bold example to answer Seamus's standing accusation: "You're sexist against men." However, this case would be challenging because there were no other cases like it—a boss suing a subordinate and his employer for sexual harassment.

189

We were pleased when the attorneys for the Getty requested that we try to settle the case in mediation—a non-binding, non-judicial, informal, and private settlement conference that takes place in an office instead of the courtroom, with a retired judge or a lawyer instead of a sitting judge. While it is expensive—the parties typically pay $500/hour and more, and up to ten thousand dollars for a single day—but there are no binding orders or judgments, and there's little downside to trying to settle a case there. There is no court reporter to make a record, and the parties do not testify or produce evidence, as they would in a trial or an arbitration. Most cases settle in mediation.

Within a few months, we were in mediation in the San Francisco offices of Tony Piazza, an elfin windsurfer in a three-piece suit. He was the big shot in the burgeoning field of private mediation and had traveled from his home on Maui to the mainland to meet with us. He charged $10,000 per day, but his track record for settling cases was extraordinary. Those who could afford him used him.

Every mediator has his or her own style. What is standard is that each party to the dispute is given their own room for the day so that they can freely discuss and debate with the mediator and each other without fear of the opposition hearing them. Then there is usually an opening session where the counsel, with or without their clients, makes a presentation of their claims and attacks the claims, express or anticipated, of the other side.

Late on the evening of that first day, we reached a settlement that was by its terms confidential, but promised that Turner could complete Volume IV of the *Drawings* catalog, and that he would receive a cash settlement before resigning. While the money was important, I was driven by the necessity of safeguarding the reputation of a renowned scholar, whose reputation the Getty wanted sullied to undermine the authority of his revelation of forgeries in the collection. The Getty insisted on a provision in the settlement requiring that any future disputes between the parties go to binding arbitration and judgment.

When a defendant pays money to settle a case, it is routine to require the plaintiff to keep the amount confidential, and to require arbitration of any future disputes. Turner was giving up his right to a jury trial in the future. I'd never liked these provisions, but it had become impossible to get settlements without them. And the most important provision of the deal was the Getty's commitment to publish Turner's Volume IV of the *Drawings* catalog, including the forgeries.

Over the next year, using the binding arbitration clause as insulation, the Getty employed its editorial process to try to bury publication of the catalog Turner had authored, and with it the revelation of the forgeries in the collection. Endless unnecessary delays appeared calculated to thwart the publication of Turner's research and writing. If the publication were to be snuffed out in the editorial process, it would permanently tarnish his reputation. The official catalog constituted the record of his years of research and writing.

Again, my letters were ignored. So I filed a new lawsuit, in court, even though I knew the Getty would insist it was legally subject to arbitration. The Getty would have to go to court to get an order sending the case to arbitration. This was our shot at public revelation—a powerful motivator for the Getty to perform under the original settlement. As a plaintiff's attorney, typically representing the less powerful party, I know that the likelihood of publicity and exposure of wrongdoing can prompt a powerful institution to come to a fair settlement. Press coverage has a way of bringing the other party to the table. This case was just such an example.

The Getty got a judge to order arbitration. In the meantime, a reporter for *The New York Times* who was researching art forgeries and looting came to interview me and Turner. When the same reporter contacted the Getty, their attorneys set about killing the story in its entirety. Getty's attorney insisted that since we were in arbitration, "She can't talk to the press! This is an arbitration, a binding one." The arbitrator responded, "Erin Brockovich was an arbitration, as I recall." The motion was denied.

The following Sunday, *The New York Times* featured our case on the Sunday magazine cover, with the headline—"Fakes?"—printed over one of the alleged forgeries.

Settlement quickly followed. Turner received another cash settlement, and Volume IV was published—with its revelation of the forgeries—finally, after years of efforts to suppress it.

An important scholar's reputation was preserved, and the Turners, who are still married today, later told me I saved their marriage.

Although the stalking subordinate remains employed at the Getty, I still think of this case as one of my proudest accomplishments in the law, one that made a real difference in someone's life. Turner acknowledged his gratitude in print by placing my name in the official Acknowledgments in his catalog. He also inscribed my signed copy as follows:

*To Peggy Garrity,*

*Without whose great efforts this catalogue would not have seen the light of day. She has brilliantly outmaneuvered the powerful forces that sought to suppress its publication . . . the book is a monument to her skills as a lawyer as well as to civil and intellectual liberty. We Turners shall be forever grateful.*

*With warmest thanks,*
*Nicholas Turner*

# CHAPTER 18

# BEST INTERESTS OF THE CHILDREN

The small Buddha sitting on the back edge of the desk caught my eye immediately as my opponent and I entered Judge Roy Paul's chambers for our first conference one morning in 2001, a few weeks after hijacked airplanes crashed into both towers of New York's World Trade Center while the whole world watched on television.

*This Buddha is a good sign*, I thought. *Judge Paul must have a spiritual side.*

Piles of court files and thick pleadings covered the desk, attesting to the magnitude of marital conflict in the Central District of Los Angeles County. This was a singularly unglamorous place, belying the media accounts of celebrity divorce proceedings. Our judge was obviously a workhorse, a saint, and maybe a Jedi. I would need him to tap into all those powers for this case, because I was representing my yoga teacher of many years and felt a keen responsibility.

I had just returned from a yoga retreat in the mountains of Utah that summer, where I'd had some profound experiences, and I felt a renewed connection to the practice and study of yoga. During the preceding decade I had studied yoga with Rod Stryker, as well as a smattering of other teachers at Yoga Works in Santa Monica, maybe the hottest yoga teacher incubator in the country. After my daughter Erin had introduced me to yoga at a much lesser studio in the late '80s, I'd become hooked, craving the centering influence of meditation in my life as a litigator and single mom. She eventually led me to regular classes at Yoga Works, and Rod.

Over the years Rod and I had become friends, and I had attended his wedding to Cheryl Tiegs—a marriage that was now the subject of these proceedings. This was Rod's first marriage. For Cheryl it was, as *People* magazine had headlined it, "THE BOTTOM OF THE FOURTH."

While I always felt tremendous responsibility to protect my client's interests, this case presented special challenges. It felt as if long-dead sages and saints of the tantric yoga tradition had dropped this case in my lap, ordaining me to take care of this young yoga master and his two baby boys, ushering them safely through the treacherous maze of Los Angeles Family Law Court. I had not been doing much family law at that point; instead, I'd been focusing on civil rights cases, especially discrimination and harassment in the workplace. The years litigating those contentious matters, I figured, prepared me for whatever battle was on the horizon—and I was certain there would be a battle.

This challenge came along around the same time as the Getty case. A seismic shift was taking place in my practice: I was representing men in my two most important cases . . . cases in which all the stereotypes were reversed. I was representing

Turner, a male supervisor, as a plaintiff in a sexual harassment case; and now Rod, the father of baby twins, in Stryker v. Tiegs, a divorce and custody case. This would have seemed impossible to me just ten years earlier, but here I was—and I relished the opportunity these cases presented to demonstrate that bias is everywhere, in each and every one of us, whether we recognize it or not, and that bias imperils all of us. I had come up against my own biases repeatedly during my years trying cases. I acknowledged this to potential jurors during jury selection in every case, and pointed out that the duty, for each of us, is to not allow our biases to influence important decisions.

Now I had much more than my own biases to reckon with.

\*　　\*　　\*

In this divorce action, Rod was leaving the marriage specifically because of Cheryl's demonstrated lack of interest in the babies. In the fourteen months since their birth, I was informed by nannies, she had bathed one of them, and only one of them, just once. It was also reported that she didn't play with them or read them bedtime stories. In fact, witnesses told me, Cheryl spent more time with the twins during the one-day photo shoot she did with them for *People* magazine when they were about six months old than she had in the preceding six months of their lives. After the shoot she had the designer nursery in the photos dismantled and the babies moved to the far end of her Bel Air mansion. Rod didn't want to take the babies away from a mother who wanted them. On the contrary, she didn't seem to want them. He just wanted to make sure they had a truly nurturing environment in which to grow up. It hadn't dawned on him to request sole custody. But, as unusual as it was, the decision was obvious to me as a litigator.

Based upon the facts as I understood them, I recommended that Rod request sole custody in his divorce filing. There was no other way to guarantee that the babies would receive the care they needed at all times. If a mother shows no interest in her babies, I felt, it would be damaging to them to be exposed to that even on a part-time basis. The question was whether Cheryl really wanted to, and would, parent them. And the evidence indicated otherwise.

Like the push toward privatization in the civil courts, there had been recent developments in family law that I found worked against people's best interests, including the gradual elimination of live testimony. The presumption seemed to be that either everyone was lying or everyone was telling the truth—or that it just didn't matter. Increasingly, judges were making decisions based upon written declarations, without the truth serum of cross-examination. Cases were "heard" in increments of a few hours, on non-consecutive days, often spread over months, depriving the parties of the continuity and momentum required to present evidence to prove their case. "Trying" a case in family law court was a bit like riding a bicycle on deflated tires: you had a bike, but it wouldn't take you anywhere. These developments seemed designed to relieve the court of much of its responsibility, and to allow lawyers and parties to drag cases out endlessly and at great expense to the parties. It also encouraged parties and counsel to hire private judges.

Because of this, a small circle of certified family law attorneys, assisted by a similarly small circle of psychiatrists on a court-approved list and, increasingly, private "rent-a-judges" who were paid $500/hour and up to handle these cases out of sight of the public, were becoming the norm. These overlapping circles of professionals had developed very cozy relationships that economically benefited those in the circle.

Essentially, a taxpayer-financed court system designed to

provide equal access for all, rich and poor alike, was becoming privatized for the wealthy, at the expense of everyone else. Experienced judges, whose experience came at taxpayer expense in taxpayer-funded courtrooms, were leaving the bench in droves for the much more lucrative private judging businesses. At the same time, courthouses were becoming dangerously underfunded, reducing the number of judges and courtrooms available to the rest of the public, and imperiling the entire system. The less affluent were being left with poorly maintained courthouses and overworked and underpaid judges. Equal justice for all had become a quaint notion.

In my opinion, however, the most disturbing and mischief-making development in family law was the statute providing that a finding of domestic violence established a legal presumption against custody in the parent guilty of the violence. That sounds logical on its face; however, it became just another weapon in many cases. The statute generated a cottage industry for lawyers who could build a custody case on such a finding—and that required him or her to first get such a finding. Sadly, this scenario became a routine part of many custody cases, and, consequently, even serious domestic violence cases were suspect. Even the nicest people are at their worst in the pressure cooker of family law court.

A classic Los Angeles problem faced us. The mother in this case was a former "super model," a media celebrity well versed in management of the press to her advantage. She needed to avoid the negative publicity a loss of custody would bring, even though, we would learn shortly, she didn't want custody in the first place. Her attorney was a prominent family law specialist—and, he quickly informed me, head of the Beverly Hills bar family law section. He knew all the players, having had ongoing interactions with the judges, the private judges, and the psychiatrists.

His firm, like other family law specialists, actually marketed their services as "specializing in high net worth clients." It was what my old circle at Coco's would have howled over as a "lawyer joke."

While the issue of child custody should be driven by the needs of the child, it has been increasingly driven by economics in recent years. The more custodial time a parent has with a child, the less likely it is that parent will have to pay child support to the other parent—so the higher-income parent is likely to be advised by her attorneys to seek the maximum amount of custody, to minimize the amount of support she is likely to be ordered to pay. This is, in my opinion, a big part of the current and ridiculous joint custody paradigm, which is marketed with the truism, "Kids need both parents." Parental rights and economic considerations have been elevated above the best interests of the child in many cases, and with a routine joint custody order, the courts are relieved of their burden to dig into the facts of the case and make difficult decisions.

Pursuing sole custody was not something I did just because my client wanted it, nor was it merely a power play on his part. There was good evidence from nannies and other household staff that Cheryl had not bonded with the babies and spent no time caring for them. There was also a record to indicate that Cheryl used scorched-earth tactics in all three of her previous divorces, including vindictively destroying important parts of the photo archives of her former husband, the world-renowned photographer Peter Beard. In my gut, I knew something was coming.

It shouldn't have been a surprise, I guess, when Cheryl and her counsel contrived to set Rod up on a bogus domestic violence accusation, which had the potential to destroy his life's work as well as our case.

Judge Paul looked disturbed on our first morning in court when he learned that Cheryl had installed a "bodyguard" in the house who had provocatively stepped between the babies and their father one evening when Rod arrived home from a yoga retreat. The game plan, I concluded, was to assert bogus domestic violence charges against my client should he challenge the "bodyguard." Judge Paul saw through the scheme immediately, observing that there was no evidence that the yoga teacher had any history of violence. He ordered that the "bodyguard" stay at least one hundred feet away from Rod at all times, and then set up a schedule for shared custody until trial. This temporary order was not unreasonable under these circumstances, involving little babies, and our judge was giving thoughtful consideration to the matter before him, which was limited to temporary orders regarding custody. The system seemed to be working, so far.

Cheryl, always dressed in azure blue, which I started to wear to court appearances myself, was accurately described in one of the tabloids as furious at the judge's order, slamming her fist on the counsel table where she sat. That same tabloid stationed paparazzi with telephoto lenses outside the mansion a few days later to shoot photos of my client moving his belongings out with the help of a few friends. He had agreed to move out as part of the temporary arrangement and order.

As expected, we were referred to a court-appointed psychiatrist for a custody evaluation and recommendation next. We had no illusions that the recommendation would be for anything but joint custody, and we were right: after many hours of interviews and observation over several months, and payment of $30,000 ($15,000 from each party), the recommendation was for joint custody.

Before the psychiatric evaluation was finalized in a written recommendation, two of the nannies called Rod to report that they had lied to the custody evaluators because Cheryl had threatened them with severe consequences if they didn't do as she instructed them. These young women took a huge risk in contacting Rod and admitting to having lied to the evaluators—and they were adamant that the children would be at risk if left with Cheryl, even in a joint custody arrangement. One of them even said she was willing to testify, insisting, "You can't leave them with her. You're the only one who gives them any love and attention. You're the only parent they have."

During the months of joint custody between the first court appearance and the trial date, Cheryl showed almost no interest in the babies; she didn't even come to the door to greet them when Rod returned them to her. Instead she had them delivered to the back door, where nannies would take them to their room. She once returned the two sixteen-month olds to Rod's home alone, without car seats, in a chauffeured limousine. Several nannies had quit, they told me, because of the way Cheryl ignored the babies.

For Rod, stipulation to joint custody was out of the question now, especially after the call from the nannies.

With a trial date approaching shortly after Labor Day, we notified the court of our rejection of the report's joint custody recommendation and our intention to go to trial. Cheryl, who was vacationing in the Hamptons, wanted the trial date continued and, in the interim, to have the eighteen-month-old babies sent to her, like cargo, for two weeks. Her attorneys seemed dumbfounded when we declined.

Momentum is important in litigation, whether in a civil case or family court, so getting to trial as quickly as possible is best for the party in the right. And in this case we had real urgency in getting to trial because of the special vulnerability of the babies, as reported by the nannies. We prepared for trial.

And then, against my vehement advice, Rod called Cheryl to discuss settlement. She did not want to return to Los Angeles for trial and did not want custody of the babies. She made clear what she wanted was to get out from under any financial responsibility for them and Rod agreed to relieve her of that burden. He ignored my warnings of this being used to show he wanted her out of the babies' lives, and continued talking with her. He wanted peace, and it sounded as if she did too.

Cheryl's attorneys and I went back and forth and got nowhere. Two days before trial, Rod contacted Cheryl again and she told him, through tears, "My attorney won't let me. He doesn't want to lose this case."

Rod and Cheryl continued to talk—and finally, on the day set for trial, we reached a settlement agreement that gave Rod sole custody, and Cheryl visitation and a release from liability for child support.

Since liability for child support can't legally be waived in California, Cheryl's lawyers crafted a contractual mechanism that amounted to the same thing. Unlike child support, spousal support is subject to contract. So her attorneys crafted a provision in the agreement that would automatically trigger an order for Rod to pay spousal support to Cheryl in the identical amount of child support that she might be ordered to pay. As a matter of law, however, she could still be held legally responsible for their care and support if Rod died.

That remote possibility was erased a few years later when Rod married a beautiful and maternal young woman named Gina who the boys had called "Momma" for nearly five years. Gina and Rod filed for stepparent adoption so Gina would become in the eyes of the law what she had already become in the eyes of the boys: their real mother. Cheryl signed away her parental rights to the boys, whom she had not seen or requested to see since the divorce, and was for once and for all guaranteed immunity from any possible responsibility for the boys, financial or otherwise. The best interests of the children won out after all.

# CHAPTER 19

# AN UNHOLY ALLIANCE

I hadn't litigated spousal abuse cases for many years, but in 2003 two of these cases were referred to me by a women's shelter. With the family law courts once again familiar terrain, I accepted them, in denial of the fact that the reason I had stopped doing family law cases with domestic violence in them was because of the toll they took on me. These were gut-wrenching cases with sometimes-weekly emergency court appearances to manage custody and visitation issues over the weekends. To take these cases was to step into the middle of the fight—at least, it was the way I did them.

In one case, Bob, a man with a martial arts black belt was not only terrorizing his wife, Shelly, with physical and psychological abuse, he was also controlling her by exploiting his knowledge of the courts and the cops. Abusers had gotten good at this tactic, understanding that a parent found guilty of domestic violence faced a presumption against getting custody, and that affected the award of child support. One day, after Bob had beaten her, Shelly went for the phone. Bob grabbed it and he made the call to the police himself, reporting that Shelly had come at him with a knife. Shelly left and went to a neighbor's to await their arrival. When she saw the squad car pull up, she returned home to find her husband reporting that he had been forced to defend himself. One of the cops, playing Solomon, informed the couple that if both made charges, and neither backed down, both would be charged and arrested and the little boy would be taken to child protective services, foster care. Horrified, Shelly declined to press charges, and the cops left. Her husband chortled.

Since the criminal process offered Shelly no hope, the therapist at the shelter had advised Shelly that her best option was to seek protection in the family law courts, where she could obtain restraining and custody orders.

Getting these orders was just the first step. Bob ignored the orders, so I had to file contempt proceedings to enforce them. When Bob was found guilty of contempt, Shelly was deliriously happy and sang to herself all the way down five floors of escalators, "Guilty, guilty, guilty."

While I understood her delight at this bit of justice, gloating like this put her at risk of his wrath and back in the dynamics of the game. Even with that win, I needed to deprogram Shelly—to arm her—so she could resist getting sucked back in when Bob came calling again, as he surely would. Spousal abuse happens in cycles, and both people play a role. Now that she was feeling safer, I worried that Shelly was again at risk of dropping her guard. Statistics show that the most dangerous time for a spousal abuse victim is when she first leaves the abuser. So, in addition to providing legal assistance, I tried to retrain my client to help her disengage from the back-and-forth with her abuser. I used role-playing to do this, and acted out manipulations Bob had used in the past, like showing up at her door unannounced to get something that young Sam had forgotten. She had let him in even after we got the first order.

I resorted to a kind of brainwashing. In one scenario I pretended to be Bob calling from out in front of the house: "Shelly, help me. I need your help. I've been hit by a truck and I'm lying out here under the wheels. Please, honey."

Of course, this was ridiculous, and we both laughed at the absurdity, but it helped Shelly understand the absurdity of the actual abuse dynamic at a gut level. Then I said, like a voice in her head, "Bob is calling from under a big truck that has just run over him in front of your house, begging for you to come help him. What do you do?"

Shelly was ready and said the words, "I do not go out. I call 911." We rehearsed this and other scenarios each and every time I saw her in my office. We rehearsed until I, and more importantly Shelly, believed she could pull it off.

Then there were the cases where I became the abuser's target. In only a few cases did I have genuine concern for my safety, and Ellen's case was one of those.

Ellen and her husband, Dick, had a seriously autistic little boy who required round-the-clock care and monitoring. Ellen had given up her lucrative job to provide care for their son, and she worked to keep his environment as calm as possible. Overstimulation of any kind, especially noise, could send Sam into a violent and self-destructive state. But even though he knew this, Dick would become angry and throw things, smashing mirrors and lamps within feet of Ellen and Sam.

By the time I got the case, it had been in the courts for months. Ellen's previous attorney, her second one, had just bowed out because of threats Dick had made against her; she had taken a Krav Maga self-defense course, and she still feared for her safety. I substituted in as attorney of record for Ellen, but only after she promised to do everything I asked of her without question. I was finally, I thought, beyond risking my own well-being without such a commitment from my client. But I had not properly assessed the risk of the abuser taking aim at me—not literally, anyway—or of his cunning.

My appearance in the case presented a threat to Dick's pathological need for control over his wife and his home. I think he reasoned, *I've already driven off two law firms, so why not the next one too?*

He left daily threatening phone messages like, "Think of me when you start your car"; "Next time you are in court I'm going to smash your face into the glass door"; and "You won't know when it's coming, but when it does it will be me, and you deserve it." He taunted me with knowledge about past cases I had tried, demeaning me the way he demeaned his wife. "You were just lucky, Garrity, a flash in the pan. You're done. I know all about you. I will ruin you." Occasionally, he was comical, like New Years Day 2003 when he left me the following message: "Happy New Year. I got screwed by you in 2002. You'll get screwed by me in 2003."

I never actually spoke to this madman, who did other amusing things like purchase five new designer suits at Saks, charge them to his brother, have them altered, and then never pick them up. My personal favorite was his somehow draining $30,000 out of his own attorney's bank account. The unctuous attorney, who was a much-published legal writer and expert on father's rights, had insisted that poor Dick was the abused one.

I brought in the brilliant and witty security expert Gavin de Becker to assess the severity of the threat and to advise me on ways to minimize my risk. Gavin, author of the *New York Times* bestseller *The Gift Of Fear,* had been our forensic expert on the Teak Dyer wrongful death case years earlier. His specialty was threat assessment. I followed his instructions to the letter as Ellen and I fought for and got all the orders we sought, including control over the family money and assets. Dick never showed up in court, however, until he was arrested on a criminal warrant and appeared in handcuffs and jailhouse orange. When his family had him extradited to the US from Australia. The extradition was a move they would all regret. Everyone had been safer with Dick out of the country.

In the summer of 2003 I had to hire Gavin a third time, now to investigate and protect me from my own secretary, a woman named Carolyn, who, unbeknownst to me, was a convicted felon and scheming thief who had plotted against a number of her past employers like a bank robber plots against a bank. In one case, while working for a car rental company, she stole a car. In another she set up a false disability claim against one of the big law firms. She combined those skills and both stole a car from and made false claims for benefits against me.

I had relied on an employment agency to screen her when I hired her in 2002. They had not done so, although they had collected a $7,500 fee from me.

Carolyn quit work abruptly one day—while I was out of the office, and just after I had completed mediation of a sexual harassment suit. The mediator and the attorneys were in the process of finalizing a settlement. The following day I received a call from the mediator telling me the other side was calling off the settlement because of some dramatic new evidence. Shortly thereafter, I received a letter by messenger from opposing counsel informing me that Carolyn had offered to testify that my client and I had fabricated the entire case. They were going to use her testimony in court, and insisted that I could not stop them by asserting violation of attorney client privilege for two reasons: First, they said, it couldn't violate attorney client privilege if I was asserting that what she said she had heard was never said. Second, they asserted that what she was accusing me and my client of was a fraud and a crime, and that therefore the privilege did not apply.

When a judge seemed to be seriously considering allowing Carolyn to give such shocking testimony, without questioning the ethics of the law firm offering the testimony of a secretary from another law firm, all my years of faith in the legal system dissolved. If she were allowed to testify, it wouldn't matter whether the testimony was false or not. The wounds inflicted on both me and my client would be fatal. The accusation alone would destroy my reputation and force me off the case.

My client would have to find another lawyer who was willing to step into the line of fire at the last possible moment with nothing to gain for himself. Boy, did I have one. I phoned Tom Girardi, who'd won billions in the Erin Brockovich cases and occasionally tormented opposing corporate counsel by buying their Gulfstream jets out from under them.

Without my even getting the story out, Tom said, "Send it over"—and I knew I was going to be okay, and that my client would be too. This is the kind of camaraderie and kinship that exists among the plaintiffs' bar that scares the hell out of the corporate bullies. Trial lawyers stick together for each other and, most importantly, for average people who need lawyers to take on the bullies.

I was still in the fight of my life to save my reputation and my law license.

Within a few hours, Gavin discovered Carolyn's grand theft auto felony conviction. Funny, because she had taken a car of mine she had persuaded me to allow her to drive while she was "buying" it with deductions from her paycheck. Of course, there could be no deductions if there was no paycheck. For extra devilment, she'd taken along with her the computer backup tapes on all the office files.

It got worse.

Carolyn soon contacted defense counsel on all my pending cases with similar schemes. When I learned this, I had to notify all clients that their cases might have been compromised, and that I would likely have to withdraw as their counsel. This resulted in numerous lost clients and huge financial losses. What little faith in the system I still harbored vanished when I learned that none of my colleagues in the defense bar who had been approached had felt ethically compelled to warn me of the threat to my practice, my clients, and even the integrity of the legal system in Los Angeles, where temporary secretaries go from firm to firm. I happened upon this shocking information through a former client, not from members of the bar.

After securing good orders from the judge, and before Dick was dragged into court on the extradition, I'd felt that my client and her son were safe, and that any threat to me from that case was over. It was not.

I found a message on my phone one morning from Dick: "Nice try, but I am way ahead of you . . . Not going to fall for it." Next I received a very recent e-mail exchange between him and Carolyn in which she offered to "help" him. She proposed a case against me with the state bar of California. Dick crowed in his forwarding e-mail that he had outsmarted me, figuring Carolyn's invitation was all a trick I had come up with to ensnare him. Occasionally, in these dark moments, the universe seemed to give me a laugh to keep me going.

I expended hundreds of hours and most of the following year defending myself against false claims Carolyn made against me to the Labor Relations Board, the Department of Fair

Employment and Housing, Workers Compensation, and other agencies. I learned she had been unsuccessful in recruiting any lawyer to sue me for race discrimination, so at least some of my reputation was still intact.

The wear and tear on my body mounted, however, until I was depleted and the jig was up. I suffered fatigue and went to an acupuncturist for abdominal pain that I figured was stress-related. She treated me with needles and strong Chinese herbs—which, it turned out, might have been worse than no treatment.

Before dawn on the morning of November 30, 2004, my daughter, Erin, who just happened to have come out to Malibu the night before to have dinner with me, found me doubled over and walking around the living room, crying, "I'm dying . . . I'm dying." I had been up all night trying, irrationally, to meditate the pain away, and I did not want to wake her until I could stand it no longer. I was used to sucking up pain at this point in my life, as it seemed a constant.

Now it was Erin's turn to take care of me.

# CHAPTER 20

# MY NEAR-DEATH EXPERIENCE

Erin rushed me to the emergency room of St. John's Hospital, where the nurses, one of whom I saw crying, told her to summon the rest of the family immediately and advise them that my life was in danger. I was septic, with my systems starting to shut down—most dramatically, my heart.

Erin, my sweet girl, had calmly navigated through early rush-hour traffic on Pacific Coast Highway, with me moaning in the passenger seat. When I'd demanded to be let out of the car to be sick on the side of the road at Topanga Canyon, she'd reached into the backseat, opened a package of new bedsheets she was going to return, and held them up around me to shield me from view. Then she'd very carefully helped me back into the car.

Every move was excruciating. When we arrived at the ER of St. John's, I refused to sit in a wheelchair and hobbled along instead, bent over like Hansel and Gretel's witch.

While I was in the emergency room and being given morphine intravenously, the surgeon on call arrived to let me know I had an extremely irregular EKG.

"I think you have had a heart attack," he said.

I wondered aloud why he was telling me this and not just fixing whatever needed fixing . . . until he showed me a CT scan revealing a perforated colon and peritonitis. Evidently I had greater problems at the moment than even this EKG. They were preparing me for surgery to fix my intestines after an all-day effort to stabilize me—and to let me be with my family for perhaps the last time, although no one told me that part.

I was in surgery for eight hours and then ICU for ten days. My kids demanded that Dr. Uyeda, the surgeon, tell them I was going to be okay, and they fell apart when he refused and instead said, "Her life is in danger and we won't know for several weeks whether she will live. This kind of infection is usually fatal. So far, she has survived the surgery."

My surgeon would later tell me, "You're a real stoic. Most people would have gotten to the doctor a lot sooner with that kind of pain."

I certainly didn't consider myself a stoic; in fact, I felt like a big baby whenever I was sick. For me, any sickness I suffered was a sign of weakness, something I had to deny to myself until it could not be denied. Now my treatment required numerous doctors, internists, gastroenterologists, a cardiac specialist, infectious disease specialists, surgeons, and a psychiatrist. And the grace of God. I could just imagine lawyer jokes like, "Do we really have to save a trial lawyer? See, they really are full of shit." Instead, I received remarkable and thorough care from everyone who treated me, including my amazing nurses. And it turned out my surgeon was about to take the California bar himself, so we shared camaraderie on that front later on.

For the first week I was simply out of my head, delirious a good deal of the time. Mom had died six weeks earlier, and one day she appeared to me in the doorway of my room. Extending her hand, she said firmly, "Come with me." As she did, another woman I couldn't see who was sitting right next to me grabbed my arm and said just as firmly, "You're not going anywhere."

I didn't really care whether I left with my mother or not. Then suddenly I was back in my bed, writhing in pain, with an open wound the length of my belly and multiple intravenous lines in my arms. Tubes and blinking monitors were everywhere. My body was immobilized; the only reason the doctors had agreed not to use actual restraints was because my kids promised to monitor me round the clock. I was restless in the extreme, and I tried to pull out the lines and escape from the bed. I would require a second surgery eight months later and a lot of medical care going forward.

I would also require one more trip to court to defend myself against Carolyn's false charges, this time with a lawyer representing me. To my astonishment, the case was assigned to Judge Roy Paul, who was now assigned to the court in Long Beach. I felt safe, even protected by grace, immediately. This was the remarkable jurist who had seen through the chicanery in the Stryker–Tiegs divorce in downtown Los Angeles several years before. He saw through it here, too, and made Carolyn listen several times to her taped phone threat to me, left the day she walked out, which proved she had fabricated the case.

What about my law practice? I would have to figure that out later.

In the preceding year, after Carolyn had decimated my practice, I had taken on some sketchy clients against my own best judgment. Incredibly but perhaps predictably, these same clients refused to release me from their cases now that I was sick. One even demanded to be told where I was hospitalized, and had her therapist, who had referred her to me, call me in my first week at home and press me to stay on the case. Apparently

I had convinced these people that I was indestructible. I would have to find a lawyer to go into court for me and argue for my release in the several remaining cases. Fortunately, once again, I had one nearby.

My friend, confidante, and professional compatriot, Marcia Clark, who sat with me every day I was in the hospital and had stayed with my kids while they awaited the outcome of the surgery, offered to go to court for me though she hadn't seen the inside of a civil courtroom in decades. She and I had spent hours together on the golf course, swearing at bad putts—and, I teased her, "looking for the real killer." It was my indelicate reference to her prosecution of O.J. Simpson, who had, of course, been acquitted of slaughtering his ex-wife Nicole Brown Simpson. Once, as Marcia hunted around the rough on the other side of the green for the ball she had overshot, she came up holding a brand-new white golf glove, men's size large, and said, sheepishly, "Look what I found. I just can't turn this in, but someone is going to be missing it. You do it." I doubled over with laughter and couldn't wait to see the face of the guy in the pro shop when I turned the glove in and reported what had happened.

Now winged by illness, I was so grateful that Marcia would step in for me without hesitation. I joked that she didn't know how to do anything except ask for a conviction and the death penalty—and I said I was counting on her to do just that with the jokers on the other side of the case who were insisting that I remain on the case or prove to them why I couldn't. If it were not for Marcia's constant support and good humor, and the amazing love and prayers of my family, yoga teacher, and friends, I don't think I could have made it through this, or would have wanted to.

In the ensuing months I had to rely on my spiritual life to sustain me. With an open wound I could not do any kind of yoga *asana*, the physical poses, so I turned to the non-physical practices of the tradition, including meditation and *yoga nidra*. In this ancient practice a person creates a personalized *sankalpa,* a resolution to actualize a desired goal, and does visualizations to achieve that goal and break the hold of their subconscious resistance.

While I was still unconscious, Rod placed a unique little statue of a dancing Ganesh by my bedside and did a special healing meditation with Seamus. He also contacted yogis of our tradition in the Himalayas, who joined in. Other people from various religious and spiritual traditions, from fundamental Christians in Southern California to Catholic nuns in Wisconsin, simultaneously stormed heaven with prayers for my healing. There is no doubt in my mind that the prayers, meditations, and spiritual practices performed on my behalf were instrumental in my survival.

# CHAPTER 21

# KEEPING THE FAITH

On a warm summer evening in 2007, during one of my long-distance cocktail hours with my younger sister, Sheila—featuring Waterford tumblers of Jameson's on both ends—I expressed how depressed I felt having had to give up my law practice. I felt powerless to contribute anything meaningful to the world. Because of my compromised immune system, I was afraid of getting deathly sick again, so I'd just declined an invitation to go with a group from my church in Santa Monica to an orphanage in Mexico to deliver clothes, toys, and other necessities.

Sheila decided to step in. She challenged me to fly back to the Midwest the coming weekend for a few days at her place on the Mississippi River. "You should be here," she said, crisply, as she always did, emphasizing certain syllables to generate guilt, and others to remind me that I was the family runaway. She proposed we join a civil rights march in support of jailed Guatemalan immigrants and their families that was being organized by the Franciscan nuns at St. Rose Convent in La Crosse, Wisconsin. She would take care of everything, she explained. I would simply have to follow her instructions. She would pick me up at the airport and I would spend the next few days at her mercy.

A violent raid by Immigration and Customs Enforcement (ICE) on a kosher meatpacking plant had decimated tiny Post-ville, Iowa (population 2,000) a few months earlier. Over one-third of the population had been arrested. Showcasing hundreds of heavily armed federal agents (two for every arrestee), swarms of black helicopters, and convoys of black SUVs and prison buses, this arm of Homeland Security had swooped in and demonstrated its might by rounding up immigrant slaughterhouse workers. The immigrants, most of whom were no taller than five feet, were illiterate, spoke no English, and had been brought to Iowa by the New York owners of the plant.

After their arrest, the immigrants were chained—hand, foot, and waist, as well as to each other—and hauled like animals to the National Cattle Congress Fairgrounds in Waterloo, Iowa.

Once there, armed federal agents herded these illiterate Guatemalan peasants down cattle chutes and into trailers set up as "continuance of operations" courts for stage-managed and expedited arraignment, where they coerced guilty pleas to manufactured felony crimes, then subjected the men to summary conviction and sentencing to federal prisons around the country. After serving prison time, the immigrants would be deported, something they would have agreed to at the time of their arrests, and which would have saved taxpayers the more than $5,000,000 it cost to incarcerate them all. I tried to imagine the terror these indigenous Mayan people must have felt.

These entire proceedings were completed in less than two weeks before federal judges handpicked by the Bush administration. Translators, flown in from around the country, learned it was a top priority national security exercise. Cameras and recording devices were not allowed. Erik Camayd-Freixas, PhD, a professor of Spanish at Florida International University and one of the translators summoned to this "exercise," was so horrified by what he saw that he broke the code of silence observed by court interpreters in a lengthy essay, "Interpreting After the Largest ICE Raid in US History: A Personal Account," which he circulated among the other two dozen interpreters at his university. The essay became a sensation and was covered by *The New York Times* and numerous other publications, and was later invoked in demands for comprehensive immigration reform.

In May 2009, too late to help the Postville workers who had served prison terms and been deported, the US Supreme Court declared it illegal for US Attorneys to use felony charges of identity theft to leverage a guilty plea in immigration cases.

In 2007, our caravan from St. Rose Convent snaked across the Mississippi River over a rickety old metal suspension bridge at Lansing, Iowa, a small fishing hamlet upriver from Prairie du Chien. During the fifties this had been a Huck Finn–like kid's world where we fished, made rafts, and routinely found buried Native American arrowheads. My brothers shot each other with BB guns in hidden villages they built up, and threatened to toss us off the top of a huge boulder if we ever told on them.

As a girl "river rat" I fancied myself alternately Lewis and Clark's Sacajawea or Tom Sawyer's Becky, realizing even at that young age that I had to make the gender thing work for me. We made the most of our lack of parental supervision in ways that scare me, looking back—literally risking life and limb as we played along the river. I remember dancing across the wooden railroad bridge, bouncing from tie to tie almost thirty feet above the river, oblivious to the danger of either the river or the trains. One of my brothers ultimately burned that bridge down (something I learned only in adulthood).

During our trip over the bridge all these years later, I conjured up my five-year-old self, sitting in the deep velvety backseat of our old green 1952 Packard, my dad at the wheel. Overcome by deep nostalgia, I held my breath, as my many siblings and I always did on those suspension bridges until the bumpata-bumpata-bumpata-bump-bump of rubber tires over section after section of webbed steel bridge turned once again to smooth pavement. On his mission across the Wisconsin state line to Iowa to buy colored oleomargarine (illegal then in "America's Dairyland"), my dad thought it hilarious to slow to a near stop in the middle of the bridge as the mob of us in the backseat turned blue.

Nearly 2,000 people showed up for the march through Postville. Four diminutive Guatemalan girls, surrounded by a sea of white-haired nuns, carried signs and chanted, "Sí, se puede," as they bounced down the street, smiling broadly, like the guests of honor at a street party. The marchers included older nuns in plain street clothes, alongside a few hip younger ones sporting asymmetrical haircuts, dark leather sandals, peasant skirts, and over-the-shoulder cloth totes, looking more like art school students than nuns.

Before the march, as we started the day with Mass in the golden magnificence of St. Rose Convent's Maria Angelorum chapel, followed by breakfast in the convent dining room, I couldn't help wondering how different my life would be had I followed my urge to enter the convent after high school. I am sure that as a "bride of Christ" I would've been just as restless as I had been in my conventional marriages. But the FSPA nuns were the first real feminists I'd known as a young Catholic girl, and their communal life of spirituality and intellectual pursuits had appealed to me. As had their knowing smiles behind the backs of priestly pomposity.

Now here I was with the same cheeky nuns I'd wanted to join way back in high school, including Sister Lucille, one of their most prominent leaders, and one of the great influences of my life. She'd shooed me away to college, no doubt knowing that the convent was probably not the right place for me. When I reminded Sister Lucille of her words from long ago, she responded with a familiar and knowing smile and said, "And I was right, wasn't I?"

Things were heating up when we all met at St. Bridget's Catholic Church that morning. The main street of the tiny town was lined with passionate immigration opponents, foreigners themselves to these parts, shouting and carrying signs, including one quoting Tom Tancredo, the anti-immigration Arizona congressman. My personal favorite was a woman dressed up as the Statue of Liberty, face and hair painted green under a green crown, body covered by a green-painted sheet—all of which later melted in the rain. St. Bridget's had become a sanctuary under the watchful eye of the physically diminutive Sister Mary McCauley, who through national news coverage had become the unlikely face and voice of this particular struggle. McCauley was the very picture of calm in the middle of the storm, tough and impervious to the vicious taunts and threats of the anti-immigration zealots. She instructed us not to respond to the hecklers along the route, and we didn't. I guess she actually practiced that "turn the other cheek" stuff espoused by the original Christian some two thousand years ago.

McCauley's terrified flock was sheltered in St. Bridget's, many of the tiny women wearing heavy government-issue electronic ankle bracelets as they carried babies on their hips, all of them dressed up in their Sunday best red, white, and blue. They were models of patriotism for the country that had just torn their families apart. The women had been released to care for their children on the condition they wear these medieval-looking devices, which monitored them twenty-four hours each day. The women and the little kids smiled at us and clearly understood we were there to help them, but I wondered how they could trust anyone ever again.

The blatant display of federal excess met its match in McCauley when she took it upon herself to assert the authority of the Catholic Church and declare the church as well as the school bus as sanctuaries. She had reportedly summoned the parish priest by phone that day, insisting, "Father, we need a collar over here right now."

While the nuns had always been responsible for the schools, it seemed to me that there was something new afoot when a nun didn't hesitate to issue a command to a priest—and he followed it. Yet at the same time, Sister McCauley's words, "We need a collar over here right now," was an acknowledgment of the Church's male-dominated hierarchy. McCauley, and the priest she summoned, knew a priest would hold greater sway over federal agents than she, a nun, could.

McCauley's courage and candor in those terrifying circumstances was refreshing, and made me love these nuns all the more. To me, and many of us, the nuns are the embodiment of the one true Church.

On the edge of town a sign proclaimed Postville's pride in being the home of John R. Mott, winner of the Nobel Peace Prize in 1946 for promoting peace and Christian brotherhood across national boundaries, through organizations such as the YMCA. *How ironic*, I thought, as I imagined his disgust at the recent events. The Archbishop of Iowa spoke to the crowd packed into the church, first in Spanish, then in English, demonstrating a humility and humanity that shocked me into remembering the Church I once loved.

That day, Church and State synergized for me in a profound way that made my unorthodox life make sense. Midwestern law school professors spoke, joined in the demonstration, and participated in a beautiful non-denominational service, which also featured the children and spouses of the newly imprisoned. The parish then graciously served the rain-soaked marchers platters of homemade sandwiches, cookies, cakes, and brownies.

I was struck at how the grassroots of the Midwest seemed to have grown up. When I lived there in the fifties and sixties, outsiders of any kind were viewed with suspicion. Even the tourists, who filled the towns and villages for fall leaf tours or summer river fun and provided much-needed revenue, were resented. Today, "outsiders" with brown skin who spoke foreign languages were woven into the fabric of this community. I was awestruck.

During my visit, Sheila and I spent time on her deck watching barges and paddle-wheel riverboats passing, their calliope music hanging in the humid air. We marveled at the community of eagles, thriving after years on the endangered species list, diving for fish across the way. We paddled around sloughs and islands in a kayak, occasionally wielding our paddles to drench each other, and deftly dodged the barge traffic powering its way down the river.

Now it all made sense. My view of the world and the way I practiced law in Los Angeles all these years had deep roots in the small-town life along the river of my childhood. It was here that I had formed my opinions about justice, and here that I had realized it was not equal, or for all. It was here that I'd decided I had to take risks and do something about that. The powerful, dangerous, and ever-changing Mississippi River had become a part of me, so much so that I would always make my home alongside iconic and powerful bodies of water. In Chicago it was Lake Michigan, and in Southern California it was the Pacific Ocean.

# IN THE GAME

For as long as I could remember, I had been drawn to the excitement of the city and yearned for the day I could leave the small town behind and get into the heart of the action. Yet as a girl growing up there, I'd identified with the underdog and viewed life as a David-and-Goliath struggle. And I'd always wanted to be on the side of the biblical underdog, David.

# CHAPTER 22

# FINDING MY BALANCE

In March 2008 I found myself at Loyola Law School in Chicago, in wanton subversion of the teachings of my old oppressor, the Roman Catholic Church. This was a particularly festive time to visit Chicago, and I recalled riding on the float at the front of the St. Patrick's Day parade as a member of the Queen's court in 1966 and 1967. I was then a student at Rosary College, still considering becoming a nun. How times had changed. My life had gone in a very different direction.

I had spent the time since my brush with death in 2004 teaching yoga to women contemporaries as I pursued certification as a yoga teacher. I had closed my law office. I was still drawn to the law and its potential to set things right, but the sepsis I'd suffered, and the two eight-hour stretches of general anesthesia for my surgeries, had left me virtually unable to tolerate conflict and stress. I also found myself unable to focus for any length of time, and yoga and meditation, and teaching others, helped me.

Rod Stryker had brought us to this unlikely venue in Chicago for a weeklong advanced yoga teacher training. I didn't aspire to teach in any of the studios in the Los Angeles area. Instead, I hoped I could share with the less fortunate the yoga teachings that had likely saved my life. Recently reminded by the press that the Vatican still pronounces yoga anathema to Catholic Church doctrine, I was at once astounded and delighted when I learned our yoga teacher training would be held at Loyola, and happily plunked down the cost of a weeklong trip to Chicago. Yoga and meditation had shaped and animated my spiritual practice for more than twenty years, and I had yet to be struck by lightning. I felt as if I—a woman, a yogi, a trial lawyer—was on some kind of covert mission behind enemy lines, like a Trojan horse.

I was soaking up the familiar imagery around me—the beautiful frescoes in the recessed ornate ceilings, and the glorious statuary, including a replica of the Pieta. Was I a prodigal daughter come home? Was I brought here to finally put all the pieces of my spiritual life into a completed mosaic? I was struck in a new way by the artistic exaltation of a strong and powerful woman, the Blessed Mother Mary, in this institution so steeped in misogyny that it declared her a virgin centuries after she gave birth to Jesus.

Then I noticed much less artistic images competing for attention. Huge, museum-lighted portraits of dead cardinals lined the walls outside the conference room. Scarlet skullcaps crowned the heads of these princes of the Church. Weighty gold crosses hung over scarlet floor-length cassocks, and scarlet mozettas over knee-length, lacy white rochets sartorially marked these men as members of the College of Cardinals, which secretly elects the Pope. Displays of male authority were everywhere in Catholic institutions. I still felt their eyes following me.

For a fleeting moment I recalled the fear I felt because of the creepy priests who preyed upon me as a young girl. Then, just as quickly, that fear and shame dissolved. My life was now, finally, my own, and I embraced it, all of it, as part of my life's journey. I also embraced the humor and irony of the circumstances in which I now found myself.

I looked forward defiantly to seeing the cardinals' imperious faces each time I walked past in my body-hugging yoga clothes and bare feet, fantasizing doing cartwheels down the hall. Back in class, I enjoyed myself immensely as I stood on my head and the room turned upside down. This seemed the correct perspective on my old church.

# ACKNOWLEDGMENTS

Endless thanks to the following people, and apologies to those I may have inadvertently left out:

My daughter/editor Bronwyn Garrity, for her candor, brilliance, encouragement, and the many hours she spent in the margins and between the lines; Erin Garrity; Colin Garrity; Bronwyn Garrity; Seamus Garrity, for your love, tolerance, patience, and great material, and for my grandchildren—Carys, Graham, Charlotte, Kea Lani, Vera, and Eamon; Maureen Murdock and my sister writers, Carolyn Butcher, Deb Gunther, Olivia Harris, Genie Hoyne, Hilary Klein, Hilary Krieger, Peggy Lamb, Wendy Lukomski, and Vicki Riskin, for their candor and support; Rod Stryker, for his friendship and the teachings and wisdom he so generously shared; Geri Spieler; Deanne Stillman; Sheila Garrity; Bridget Garrity; Maura Garrity; Roswitha Newman-Boss; Maryann Rimoin; Gina Stryker; Theo, Jaden, Asha, and Attreya Stryker; Virginia Harper; Valerie Cummings; Nicholas and Jane Turner; Sister Mary Linus/Lucille Winnike and the

Franciscan Sisters of Perpetual Adoration, the first feminists in my life; Maruia Jorda; Herb Colden; Dr. Mike Garrity; Maryann Garrity; Pandit Rajmani Tigunait and Shelly Craigo; Reverend Maudell Tooks; Scott Woolley; Ann Ryan; Teddy Altman; Dale Norman; Gloria Huber; Karen Riordan; Johnnie Munchkin; Judy Rosener; Margarita and Maria Santiago; Linda Burgess; Cheryl Cornett; Elaine Hall; Sara Gepp; Mona Shafer Edwards; Marcia Clark; Gavin de Becker; and Randy Newman.

# ABOUT THE AUTHOR

Peggy Garrity grew up in the Mississippi River hamlet of Prairie du Chien, Wisconsin, population 6,000—a town with two Catholic churches, four Catholic schools, and fifty bars and pubs. After attending night law school for five years and having three babies, she was admitted to the California State Bar in December 1975, and soon went on to launch a solo practice. She retired from the full-time practice of law in December, 2004, but remains committed to the law through her writing, consulting, legal commentary, and handling a few select civil rights cases.

Garrity also teaches yoga and meditation privately. The *LA Times* published her op-ed about the Halliburton rape cases, "About that Day In Court," in 2008, and she is currently at work on her next book—a legal thriller, *Justice Delayed*. Garrity is a doting grandmother of six.

*Author photo by Marisa Leigh*

# SELECTED TITLES FROM SHE WRITES PRESS

She Writes Press is an independent publishing company founded to serve women writers everywhere. Visit us at www.shewritespress.com.

*Tasting Home: Coming of Age in the Kitchen* by Judith Newton. $16.95, 978-1-938314-03-2. An extraordinary journey through the cuisines, cultures, and politics of the 1940s through 2011, complete with recipes.

*All the Ghosts Dance Free: A Memoir* by Terry Cameron Baldwin. $16.95, 978-1-63152-822-4. A poetic memoir that explores the legacy of alcoholism and teen suicide in one woman's life—and her efforts to create an authentic existence in the face of that legacy.

*Learning to Eat Along the Way* by Margaret Bendet. $16.95, 978-1-63152-997-9. After interviewing an Indian holy man, newspaper reporter Margaret Bendet follows him in pursuit of enlightenment and ends up facing demons that were inside her all along.

*Insatiable: A Memoir of Love Addiction* by Shary Hauer. $16.95, 978-1-63152-982-5. An intimate and illuminating account of corporate executive—and secret love addict—Shary Hauer's migration from destructive to healthy love.

*The Full Catastrophe: A Memoir* by Karen Elizabeth Lee. $16.95, 978-1-63152-024-2. The story of a well educated, professional woman who, after marrying the wrong kind of man—twice—finally resurrects her life.

*Uncovered: How I Left Hassidic Life and Finally Came Home* by Leah Lax. $16.95, 978-1-63152-995-5. Drawn in their offers of refuge from her troubled family and promises of eternal love, Leah Lax becomes a Hassidic Jew—but ultimately, as a forty-something woman, comes to reject everything she has lived for three decades in order to be who she truly is.